MznLnx

Missing Links Exam Preps

Exam Prep for

Intermediate Algebra

McKeague, 6th Edition

The MznLnx Exam Prep is your link from the texbook and lecture to your exams.
The MznLnx Exam Preps are unauthorized and comprehensive reviews of your textbooks.

All material provided by MznLnx and Rico Publications (c) 2010
Textbook publishers and textbook authors do not particpate in or contribute to these reviews.

MznLnx

Rico
Publications

Exam Prep for Intermediate Algebra
6th Edition
McKeague

Publisher: Raymond Houge
Assistant Editor: Michael Rouger
Text and Cover Designer: Lisa Buckner
Marketing Manager: Sara Swagger
Project Manager, Editorial Production: Jerry Emerson
Art Director: Vernon Lowerui

Product Manager: Dave Mason
Editorial Assitant: Rachel Guzmanji
Pedagogy: Debra Long
Cover Image: Jim Reed/Getty Images
Text and Cover Printer: City Printing, Inc.
Compositor: Media Mix, Inc.

(c) 2010 Rico Publications
ALL RIGHTS RESERVED. No part of this work covered by the copyright may be reproduced or used in any form or by an means--graphic, electronic, or mechanical, including photocopying, recording, taping, Web distribution, information storage, and retrieval systems, or in any other manner--without the written permission of the publisher.

Printed in the United States
ISBN:

For more information about our products, contact us at:
Dave.Mason@RicoPublications.com

For permission to use material from this text or product, submit a request online to:
Dave.Mason@RicoPublications.com

Contents

CHAPTER 1
Basic Properties and Definitions — 1

CHAPTER 2
Equations and Inequalities in One Variable — 16

CHAPTER 3
Equations and Inequalities in Two Variables — 29

CHAPTER 4
Systems of Linear Equations and Inequalities — 46

CHAPTER 5
Exponents and Polynomials — 58

CHAPTER 6
Rational Expressions and Rational functions — 71

CHAPTER 7
Rational Exponents and Roots — 84

CHAPTER 8
Quadratic Functions — 100

CHAPTER 9
Exponential and Logarithmic Functions — 111

CHAPTER 10
Conic Sections — 122

ANSWER KEY — 125

TO THE STUDENT

COMPREHENSIVE

The *MznLnx* Exam Prep series is designed to help you pass your exams. Editors at MznLnx review your textbooks and then prepare these practice exams to help you master the textbook material. Unlike study guides, workbooks, and practice tests provided by the texbook publisher and textbook authors, *MznLnx* gives you **all** of the material in each chapter in exam form, not just samples, so you can be sure to nail your exam.

MECHANICAL

The MznLnx Exam Prep series creates exams that will help you learn the subject matter as well as test you on your understanding. Each question is designed to help you master the concept. Just working through the exams, you gain an understanding of the subject--its a simple mechanical process that produces success.

INTEGRATED STUDY GUIDE AND REVIEW

MznLnx is not just a set of exams designed to test you, its also a comprehensive review of the subject content. Each exam question is also a review of the concept, making sure that you will get the answer correct without having to go to other sources of material. You learn as you go! Its the easiest way to pass an exam.

HUMOR

Studying can be tedious and dry. MznLnx's instructional design includes moderate humor within the exam questions on occassion, to break the tedium and revitalize the brain

Chapter 1. Basic Properties and Definitions

1. _____ is a branch of mathematics concerning the study of structure, relation and quantity.
   a. Concept
   b. Algebra0
   c. Undefined
   d. Undefined

2. In plane geometry, a _____ is a polygon with four equal sides, four right angles, and parallel opposite sides. In algebra, the _____ of a number is that number multiplied by itself.
   a. Thing
   b. Square0
   c. Undefined
   d. Undefined

3. Leonardo of Pisa (1170s or 1180s – 1250), also known as Leonardo Pisano, Leonardo Bonacci, Leonardo _____, or, most commonly, simply _____, was an Italian mathematician, considered by some "the most talented mathematician of the Middle Ages."
   a. Fibonacci0
   b. Person
   c. Undefined
   d. Undefined

4. In Euclidean geometry, a _____ is moving every point a constant distance in a specified direction.
   a. Translation0
   b. Concept
   c. Undefined
   d. Undefined

5. _____ are objects, characters, or other concrete representations of ideas, concepts, or other abstractions.
   a. Thing
   b. Symbols0
   c. Undefined
   d. Undefined

6. In mathematics, a _____ is the result of multiplying, or an expression that identifies factors to be multiplied.
   a. Thing
   b. Product0
   c. Undefined
   d. Undefined

7. In mathematics, an inequality is a statement about the relative size or order of two objects. For example 14 > 10, or 14 is _____ 10.
   a. Greater than0
   b. Thing
   c. Undefined
   d. Undefined

8. In mathematics, a _____ is the end result of a division problem. It can also be expressed as the number of times the divisor divides into the dividend.
   a. Quotient0
   b. Thing
   c. Undefined
   d. Undefined

9. A _____ is the result of the addition of a set of numbers. The numbers may be natural numbers, complex numbers, matrices, or still more complicated objects. An infinite _____ is a subtle procedure known as a series.
   a. Sum0
   b. Thing
   c. Undefined
   d. Undefined

10. Equivalence is the condition of being _____ or essentially equal.
    a. Equivalent0
    b. Thing
    c. Undefined
    d. Undefined

Chapter 1. Basic Properties and Definitions

11. A _____ is a symbolic representation denoting a quantity or expression. It often represents an "unknown" quantity that has the potential to change.
    a. Thing
    b. Variable0
    c. Undefined
    d. Undefined

12. In common philosophical language, a proposition or _____, is the content of an assertion, that is, it is true-or-false and defined by the meaning of a particular piece of language.
    a. Statement0
    b. Concept
    c. Undefined
    d. Undefined

13. _____ or arithmetics is the oldest and most elementary branch of mathematics, used by almost everyone, for tasks ranging from simple daily counting to advanced science and business calculations.
    a. Arithmetic0
    b. Thing
    c. Undefined
    d. Undefined

14. An _____ is a combination of numbers, operators, grouping symbols and/or free variables and bound variables arranged in a meaningful way which can be evaluated..
    a. Thing
    b. Expression0
    c. Undefined
    d. Undefined

15. In mathematics, _____ is an elementary arithmetic operation. When one of the numbers is a whole number, _____ is the repeated sum of the other number.
    a. Thing
    b. Multiplication0
    c. Undefined
    d. Undefined

16. _____ is a mathematical operation, written a^n, involving two numbers, the base a and the exponent n.
    a. Thing
    b. Exponentiating0
    c. Undefined
    d. Undefined

17. _____ is a mathematical operation, written a^n, involving two numbers, the base a and the exponent n.
    a. Exponentiation0
    b. Thing
    c. Undefined
    d. Undefined

18. In arithmetic and algebra, when a number or expression is both preceded and followed by a binary operation, an _____ is required for which operation should be applied first.
    a. Order of operations0
    b. Thing
    c. Undefined
    d. Undefined

19. In combinatorial mathematics, a _____ is an un-ordered collection of unique elements.
    a. Concept
    b. Combination0
    c. Undefined
    d. Undefined

20. _____, either of the curved-bracket punctuation marks that together make a set of _____
    a. Parentheses0
    b. Thing
    c. Undefined
    d. Undefined

Chapter 1. Basic Properties and Definitions

21. An _____ or member of a set is an object that when collected together make up the set.
    a. Element0
    b. Thing
    c. Undefined
    d. Undefined

22. In mathematics, the _____, or members of a set or more generally a class are all those objects which when collected together make up the set or class.
    a. Thing
    b. Elements0
    c. Undefined
    d. Undefined

23. Mathematical _____ is used to represent ideas.
    a. Thing
    b. Notation0
    c. Undefined
    d. Undefined

24. A _____ is a set whose members are members of another set or a set contained within another set.
    a. Subset0
    b. Thing
    c. Undefined
    d. Undefined

25. The _____, the average in everyday English, which is also called the arithmetic _____ (and is distinguished from the geometric _____ or harmonic _____). The average is also called the sample _____. The expected value of a random variable, which is also called the population _____.
    a. Thing
    b. Mean0
    c. Undefined
    d. Undefined

26. In mathematics, a _____ function in the sense of algebraic geometry is an everywhere-defined, polynomial function on an algebraic variety V with values in the field K over which V is defined.
    a. Regular0
    b. Thing
    c. Undefined
    d. Undefined

27. In mathematics, a set is called _____ if there is a bijection between the set and some set of the form {1, 2, ..., n} where n is a natural number.
    a. Thing
    b. Finite0
    c. Undefined
    d. Undefined

28. In mathematics, a _____ occurs if there is a bijection between the set and some set of the form 1, 2, ..., n where n is a natural number.
    a. Concept
    b. Finite set0
    c. Undefined
    d. Undefined

29. In mathematics and more specifically set theory, the _____ set is the unique set which contains no elements.
    a. Empty0
    b. Thing
    c. Undefined
    d. Undefined

30. In set theory and other branches of mathematics, the _____ of a collection of sets is the set that contains everything that belongs to any of the sets, but nothing else.

Chapter 1. Basic Properties and Definitions

   a. Thing
   c. Undefined
   b. Union0
   d. Undefined

31. In mathematics, the _____ of two sets A and B is the set that contains all elements of A that also belong to B (or equivalently, all elements of B that also belong to A), but no other elements.
   a. Thing
   c. Undefined
   b. Intersection0
   d. Undefined

32. _____ is a mathematical notation for describing a set by stating the properties that its members must satisfy.
   a. Thing
   c. Undefined
   b. Set-builder notation0
   d. Undefined

33. _____ is the state of being greater than any finite real or natural number, however large.
   a. Infinite0
   c. Undefined
   b. Thing
   d. Undefined

34. In set theory, an _____ is a set that is not a finite set. Infinite sets may be countable or uncountable.
   a. Thing
   c. Undefined
   b. Infinite set0
   d. Undefined

35. In mathematics, there are several meanings of _____ depending on the subject.
   a. Degree0
   c. Undefined
   b. Thing
   d. Undefined

36. In mathematics, an _____, mean, or central tendency of a data set refers to a measure of the "middle" or "expected" value of the data set.
   a. Concept
   c. Undefined
   b. Average0
   d. Undefined

37. A _____ is a type of debt. All material things can be lent but this article focuses exclusively on monetary loans. Like all debt instruments, a _____ entails the redistribution of financial assets over time, between the lender and the borrower.
   a. Thing
   c. Undefined
   b. Loan0
   d. Undefined

38. The _____ (symbol _____) and the millibar (symbol mbar, also mb) are units of pressure.
   a. Thing
   c. Undefined
   b. Bar0
   d. Undefined

39. _____ is a way of expressing a number as a fraction of 100 per cent meaning "per hundred".
   a. Percent0
   c. Undefined
   b. Thing
   d. Undefined

40. A _____ is an illustration used in the branch of mathematics known as set theory. It shows all of the possible mathematical or logical relationships between sets.

Chapter 1. Basic Properties and Definitions 5

a. Venn diagram0   b. Thing
c. Undefined   d. Undefined

41. _____ are illustrations used in the branch of mathematics known as set theory. They show all of the possible mathematical or logical relationships between sets (groups of things).
a. Thing   b. Venn diagrams0
c. Undefined   d. Undefined

42. In Euclidean geometry, a _____ is the set of all points in a plane at a fixed distance, called the radius, from a given point, the center.
a. Thing   b. Circle0
c. Undefined   d. Undefined

43. Leonhard _____ was a pioneering Swiss mathematician and physicist, who spent most of his life in Russia and Germany.
a. Person   b. Euler0
c. Undefined   d. Undefined

44. _____ was a pioneering Swiss mathematician and physicist, who spent most of his life in Russia and Germany.
a. Person   b. Leonhard Euler0
c. Undefined   d. Undefined

45. A _____ is a simplified and structured visual representation of concepts, ideas, constructions, relations, statistical data, anatomy etc used in all aspects of human activities to visualize and clarify the topic.
a. Diagram0   b. Thing
c. Undefined   d. Undefined

46. _____ was a British logician and philosopher, who is famous for conceiving the Venn diagrams, which are used in many fields, including set theory, probability, logic, statistics, and computer science.
a. Person   b. John Venn0
c. Undefined   d. Undefined

47. In geometry, a _____ is defined as a quadrilateral where all four of its angles are right angles.
a. Thing   b. Rectangle0
c. Undefined   d. Undefined

48. _____ was a French lawyer and a mathematician who is given credit for early developments that led to modern calculus. In particular, he is recognized for his discovery of an original method of finding the greatest and the smallest ordinates of curved lines, which is analogous to that of the then unknown differential calculus.
a. Pierre de Fermat0   b. Person
c. Undefined   d. Undefined

49. In mathematics, a _____ is a statement that can be proved on the basis of explicitly stated or previously agreed assumptions.

Chapter 1. Basic Properties and Definitions

a. Theorem0
b. Thing
c. Undefined
d. Undefined

50. The _____ are the only integral domain whose positive elements are well-ordered, and in which order is preserved by addition. Like the natural numbers, the _____ form a countably infinite set. The set of all _____ is usually denoted in mathematics by a boldface Z .
    a. Thing
    b. Integers0
    c. Undefined
    d. Undefined

51. A _____ is a number that is less than zero.
    a. Thing
    b. Negative number0
    c. Undefined
    d. Undefined

52. A _____ is a one-dimensional picture in which the integers are shown as specially-marked points evenly spaced on a line.
    a. Number line0
    b. Thing
    c. Undefined
    d. Undefined

53. In mathematics, a _____ may be described informally as a number that can be given by an infinite decimal representation.
    a. Thing
    b. Real number0
    c. Undefined
    d. Undefined

54. In mathematics, the _____ of a coordinate system is the point where the axes of the system intersect.
    a. Thing
    b. Origin0
    c. Undefined
    d. Undefined

55. A _____ is a set of numbers that designate location in a given reference system, such as x,y in a planar _____ system or an x,y,z in a three-dimensional _____ system.
    a. Coordinate0
    b. Thing
    c. Undefined
    d. Undefined

56. In geometry, an _____ is a point at which a line segment or ray terminates.
    a. Endpoint0
    b. Thing
    c. Undefined
    d. Undefined

57. A frame of _____ is a particular perspective from which the universe is observed.
    a. Reference0
    b. Thing
    c. Undefined
    d. Undefined

58. A _____ is a set of possible values that a variable can take on in order to satisfy a given set of conditions, which may include equations and inequalities.
    a. Thing
    b. Solution set0
    c. Undefined
    d. Undefined

Chapter 1. Basic Properties and Definitions

59. _____ are the basic objects of study in graph theory. Informally speaking, a graph is a set of objects called points, nodes, or vertices connected by links called lines or edges.
    a. Graphs0
    b. Thing
    c. Undefined
    d. Undefined

60. In mathematics, an _____ is a statement about the relative size or order of two objects.
    a. Thing
    b. Inequality0
    c. Undefined
    d. Undefined

61. _____ interest refers to the fact that whenever interest is calculated, it is based not only on the original principal, but also on any unpaid interest that has been added to the principal.
    a. Thing
    b. Compound0
    c. Undefined
    d. Undefined

62. _____ is an adjective usually refering to being in the centre.
    a. Thing
    b. Central0
    c. Undefined
    d. Undefined

63. In mathematics, the _____ of a function is the set of all "output" values produced by that function. Given a function $f : A \to B$, the _____ of f, is defined to be the set $\{x \in B : x = f(a) \text{ for some } a \in A\}$.
    a. Thing
    b. Range0
    c. Undefined
    d. Undefined

64. _____ is a physical property of a system that underlies the common notions of hot and cold; something that is hotter has the greater _____.
    a. Thing
    b. Temperature0
    c. Undefined
    d. Undefined

65. _____ is the mathematical action of repeatedly adding or subtracting one, usually to find out how many objects there are or to set aside a desired number of objects.
    a. Counting0
    b. Thing
    c. Undefined
    d. Undefined

66. In mathematics, a _____ number is a number which can be expressed as a ratio of two integers. Non-integer _____ numbers (commonly called fractions) are usually written as the vulgar fraction a / b, where b is not zero.
    a. Rational0
    b. Thing
    c. Undefined
    d. Undefined

67. In mathematics, a _____ can mean either an element of the set {1, 2, 3, ...} (i.e the positive integers) or an element of the set {0, 1, 2, 3, ...} (i.e. the non-negative integers).
    a. Whole number0
    b. Concept
    c. Undefined
    d. Undefined

68. A _____ is a quantity that denotes the proportional amount or magnitude of one quantity relative to another.

Chapter 1. Basic Properties and Definitions

a. Ratio0
b. Thing
c. Undefined
d. Undefined

69. In mathematics, an _____ number is any real number that is not a rational number- that is, it is a number which cannot be expressed as a fraction m/n, where m and n are integers.
    a. Irrational0
    b. Thing
    c. Undefined
    d. Undefined

70. In mathematics, an _____ is any real number that is not a rational number ¡ª that is, it is a number which cannot be expressed as m/n, where m and n are integers.
    a. Thing
    b. Irrational number0
    c. Undefined
    d. Undefined

71. In mathematics, _____ are any real number that is not a rational number ¡ª that is, it is a number which cannot be expressed as m/n, where m and n are integers.
    a. Thing
    b. Irrational numbers0
    c. Undefined
    d. Undefined

72. A _____ is the part of the dividend that is left over when the dividend is not evenly divisible by the divisor.
    a. Thing
    b. Remainder0
    c. Undefined
    d. Undefined

73. In mathematics, a _____ of an integer n, also called a factor of n, is an integer which evenly divides n without leaving a remainder.
    a. Thing
    b. Divisor0
    c. Undefined
    d. Undefined

74. _____ is a natural number that has exactly two distinct natural number divisors, which are 1 and the _____ itself.
    a. Prime number0
    b. Thing
    c. Undefined
    d. Undefined

75. In mathematics, factorization (British English: factorisation) or factoring is the decomposition of an object (for example, a number, a polynomial, or a matrix) into a product of other objects, or _____, which when multiplied together give the original.
    a. Thing
    b. Factors0
    c. Undefined
    d. Undefined

76. In mathematics, a _____ number (or a _____) is a natural number that has exactly two (distinct) natural number divisors, which are 1 and the _____ number itself.
    a. Prime0
    b. Thing
    c. Undefined
    d. Undefined

77. A _____ number is a positive integer which has a positive divisor other than one or itself.

Chapter 1. Basic Properties and Definitions

    a. Thing
    b. Composite0
    c. Undefined
    d. Undefined

78. The _____ of a positive integer are the prime numbers that divide into that integer exactly, without leaving a remainder. The process of finding these numbers is called integer factorization, or prime factorization.
    a. Prime factor0
    b. Thing
    c. Undefined
    d. Undefined

79. A _____ is a numeral used to indicate a count. The most common use of the word today is to name the part of a fraction that tells the number or count of equal parts.
    a. Thing
    b. Numerator0
    c. Undefined
    d. Undefined

80. A _____ is the part of a fraction that tells how many equal parts make up a whole, and which is used in the name of the fraction: "halves", "thirds", "fourths" or "quarters", "fifths" and so on.
    a. Denominator0
    b. Concept
    c. Undefined
    d. Undefined

81. A _____ is a positive integer which has a positive divisor other than one or itself.
    a. Concept
    b. Composite number0
    c. Undefined
    d. Undefined

82. The _____ integers are all the integers from zero on upwards.
    a. Thing
    b. Nonnegative0
    c. Undefined
    d. Undefined

83. The _____ of measurement are a globally standardized and modernized form of the metric system.
    a. Units0
    b. Thing
    c. Undefined
    d. Undefined

84. In mathematics, a _____ is a mathematical statement which appears likely to be true, but has not been formally proven to be true under the rules of mathematical logic.
    a. Conjecture0
    b. Concept
    c. Undefined
    d. Undefined

85. _____, also known as _____ of Alexandria, was a Greek mathematician. His Elements is the most successful textbook in the history of mathematics. In it, the principles of geometry are deduced from a small set of axioms. His method of proving mathematical theorems by logical reasoning from accepted first principles remains the backbone of mathematics and is responsible for the field's characteristic rigor
    a. Person
    b. Euclid0
    c. Undefined
    d. Undefined

86. A _____ is defined as an integer which is the sum of the positive divisors not including the number.
    a. Thing
    b. Perfect number0
    c. Undefined
    d. Undefined

Chapter 1. Basic Properties and Definitions

87. A _____ is one of the basic shapes of geometry: a polygon with three vertices and three sides which are straight line segments.
    a. Triangle0
    b. Thing
    c. Undefined
    d. Undefined

88. _____ is the theorem stating that for any triangle, the measure of a given side must be less than the sum of the other two sides but greater than the difference between the two sides.
    a. Thing
    b. Triangle inequality0
    c. Undefined
    d. Undefined

89. _____ is a temperature scale named after the German physicist Daniel Gabriel _____ , who proposed it in 1724.
    a. Fahrenheit0
    b. Thing
    c. Undefined
    d. Undefined

90. In mathematics, and in particular in abstract algebra, the _____ is a property of binary operations that generalises the distributive law from elementary algebra.
    a. Distributive property0
    b. Thing
    c. Undefined
    d. Undefined

91. In mathematics, the multiplicative inverse of a number x, denoted 1/x or x^{-1}, is the number which, when multiplied by x, yields 1. The multiplicative inverse of x is also called the _____ of x.
    a. Thing
    b. Reciprocal0
    c. Undefined
    d. Undefined

92. In mathematics, the additive inverse, or _____ of a number n is the number that, when added to n, yields zero. The additive inverse of n is denoted −n. For example, 7 is −7, because 7 + (−7) = 0, and the additive inverse of −0.3 is 0.3, because −0.3 + 0.3 = 0.
    a. Thing
    b. Opposite0
    c. Undefined
    d. Undefined

93. _____ element of an element x with respect to a binary operation * with identity element e is an element y such that x * y = y * x = e. In particular,
    a. Thing
    b. Inverse0
    c. Undefined
    d. Undefined

94. In mathematics, the _____ inverse, or opposite, of a number n is the number that, when added to n, yields zero. The _____ inverse of n is denoted −n.
    a. Thing
    b. Additive0
    c. Undefined
    d. Undefined

95. In mathematics, the _____ of a number n is the number that, when added to n, yields zero. The _____ of n is denoted −n. For example, 7 is −7, because 7 + (−7) = 0, and the _____ of −0.3 is 0.3, because −0.3 + 0.3 = 0.
    a. Thing
    b. Additive inverse0
    c. Undefined
    d. Undefined

Chapter 1. Basic Properties and Definitions

96. In set theory and its applications throughout mathematics, _____ are a collection of sets (or sometimes other mathematical objects) that can be unambiguously defined by a property that all its members share.
   a. Classes0
   b. Thing
   c. Undefined
   d. Undefined

97. A _____ is the sum of a whole number and a proper fraction.
   a. Mixed number0
   b. Thing
   c. Undefined
   d. Undefined

98. In mathematics, the _____ inverse of a number x, denoted $1/x$ or x^{-1}, is the number which, when multiplied by x, yields 1. The _____ inverse of x is also called the reciprocal of x.
   a. Multiplicative0
   b. Thing
   c. Undefined
   d. Undefined

99. The _____ of a mathematical object is its size: a property by which it can be larger or smaller than other objects of the same kind; in technical terms, an ordering of the class of objects to which it belongs.
   a. Thing
   b. Magnitude0
   c. Undefined
   d. Undefined

100. In mathematics, the _____ (or modulus) of a real number is its numerical value without regard to its sign.
   a. Absolute value0
   b. Thing
   c. Undefined
   d. Undefined

101. The _____ is a property of multiplication or addition where the product or sum remains the same, regardless of whether or not the order of the addends or factors are changed.
   a. Commutative property0
   b. Thing
   c. Undefined
   d. Undefined

102. In abstract algebra, _____ consists of sets with binary operations that satisfy certain axioms.
   a. Grouping0
   b. Thing
   c. Undefined
   d. Undefined

103. In mathematics, _____ is a property that a binary operation can have. Within an expression containing two or more of the same associative operators in a row, the order of operations does not matter as long as the sequence of the operands is not changed.
   a. Associativity0
   b. Thing
   c. Undefined
   d. Undefined

104. In mathematics, _____ expressions is used to reduce the expression into the lowest possible term.
   a. Thing
   b. Simplifying0
   c. Undefined
   d. Undefined

105. An _____ is an equality that remains true regardless of the values of any variables that appear within it, to distinguish it from an equality which is true under more particular conditions.

a. Identity0
b. Thing
c. Undefined
d. Undefined

106. In mathematics the _____ of a set which is equipped with the operation of addition is an element which, when added to any other element x in the set, yields x.
   a. Additive identity0
   b. Concept
   c. Undefined
   d. Undefined

107. The _____ states that - a number and its additive inverse have a sum of zero (0).
   a. Concept
   b. Additive inverse property0
   c. Undefined
   d. Undefined

108. Modular arithmetic (sometimes called modulo arithmetic, or _____ because of its use in the 24-hour clock system) is a system of arithmetic for integers, where numbers "wrap around" after they reach a certain value — the modulus.
   a. Concept
   b. Clock arithmetic0
   c. Undefined
   d. Undefined

109. In geometry, an _____ of a triangle is a straight line through a vertex and perpendicular to (i.e. forming a right angle with) the opposite side or an extension of the opposite side.
   a. Altitude0
   b. Concept
   c. Undefined
   d. Undefined

110. In mathematics, a _____ is a two-dimensional manifold or surface that is perfectly flat.
   a. Plane0
   b. Thing
   c. Undefined
   d. Undefined

111. In mathematics, defined and _____ are used to explain whether or not expressions have meaningful, sensible, and unambiguous values.
   a. Undefined0
   b. Thing
   c. Undefined
   d. Undefined

112. A _____ is a landform that extends above the surrounding terrain in a limited area. A _____ is generally steeper than a hill, but there is no universally accepted standard definition for the height of a _____ or a hill although a _____ usually has an identifiable summit.
   a. Mountain0
   b. Thing
   c. Undefined
   d. Undefined

113. The _____ of a ring R is defined to be the smallest positive integer n such that $n\,a = 0$, for all a in R.
   a. Thing
   b. Characteristic0
   c. Undefined
   d. Undefined

114. In mathematics, a _____ is an ordered list of objects. Like a set, it contains members, also called elements or terms, and the number of terms is called the length of the _____. Unlike a set, order matters, and the exact same elements can appear multiple times at different positions in the _____.

Chapter 1. Basic Properties and Definitions

a. Thing
b. Sequence0
c. Undefined
d. Undefined

115. Deductive _____ is the kind of _____ in which the conclusion is necessitated by, or reached from, previously known facts (the premises).
a. Reasoning0
b. Thing
c. Undefined
d. Undefined

116. In mathematics, for a statement to be mathematically _____, such a statement must be true of all natural numbers.
a. Inductive0
b. Thing
c. Undefined
d. Undefined

117. Induction or _____, sometimes called inductive logic, is the process of reasoning in which the premises of an argument are believed to support the conclusion but do not ensure it.
a. Inductive reasoning0
b. Thing
c. Undefined
d. Undefined

118. A _____ is 360° or 2∂ radians.
a. Thing
b. Turn0
c. Undefined
d. Undefined

119. In a mathematical proof or a syllogism, a _____ is a statement that is the logical consequence of preceding statements.
a. Concept
b. Conclusion0
c. Undefined
d. Undefined

120. _____ is a sequence of numbers such that the difference of any two successive members of the sequence is a constant.
a. Thing
b. Arithmetic sequence0
c. Undefined
d. Undefined

121. _____ is a kind of property which exists as magnitude or multitude. It is among the basic classes of things along with quality, substance, change, and relation.
a. Amount0
b. Thing
c. Undefined
d. Undefined

122. _____ means in succession or back-to-back
a. Thing
b. Consecutive0
c. Undefined
d. Undefined

123. A _____ is a sequence of numbers where each term after the first is found by multiplying the previous one by a fixed non-zero number called the common ratio.
a. Geometric sequence0
b. Thing
c. Undefined
d. Undefined

Chapter 1. Basic Properties and Definitions

124. In probability theory, _____ are various sets of outcomes (a subset of the sample space) to which a probability is assigned.
- a. Thing
- b. Events0
- c. Undefined
- d. Undefined

125. A _____ is an abstract model that uses mathematical language to describe the behavior of a system. Eykhoff defined a _____ as 'a representation of the essential aspects of an existing system which presents knowledge of that system in usable form'.
- a. Thing
- b. Mathematical model0
- c. Undefined
- d. Undefined

126. In mathematics, a matrix can be thought of as each row or _____ being a vector. Hence, a space formed by row vectors or _____ vectors are said to be a row space or a _____ space.
- a. Concept
- b. Column0
- c. Undefined
- d. Undefined

127. An _____ is a straight line around which a geometric figure can be rotated.
- a. Axis0
- b. Thing
- c. Undefined
- d. Undefined

128. In astronomy, geography, geometry and related sciences and contexts, a plane is said to be _____ at a given point if it is locally perpendicular to the gradient of the gravity field, i.e., with the direction of the gravitational force at that point.
- a. Horizontal0
- b. Thing
- c. Undefined
- d. Undefined

129. A _____ is a special kind of ratio, indicating a relationship between two measurements with different units, such as miles to gallons or cents to pounds.
- a. Thing
- b. Rate0
- c. Undefined
- d. Undefined

130. In mathematics and the mathematical sciences, a _____ is a fixed, but possibly unspecified, value. This is in contrast to a variable, which is not fixed.
- a. Thing
- b. Constant0
- c. Undefined
- d. Undefined

131. The _____ rule, also known as a slipstick, is a mechanical analog computer, consisting of at least two finely divided scales , most often a fixed outer pair and a movable inner one, with a sliding window called the cursor.
- a. Slide0
- b. Thing
- c. Undefined
- d. Undefined

132. A _____ is a negotiable instrument instructing a financial institution to pay a specific amount of a specific currency from a specific demand account held in the maker/depositor's name with that institution. Both the maker and payee may be natural persons or legal entities.
- a. Thing
- b. Check0
- c. Undefined
- d. Undefined

Chapter 1. Basic Properties and Definitions 15

133. The _____ of a geographic location is its height above a fixed reference point, often the mean sea level.
 a. Elevation0
 b. Thing
 c. Undefined
 d. Undefined

134. In geometry, a line _____ is a part of a line that is bounded by two end points, and contains every point on the line between its end points.
 a. Concept
 b. Segment0
 c. Undefined
 d. Undefined

135. A _____ is a part of a line that is bounded by two end points, and contains every point on the line between its end points.
 a. Thing
 b. Line segment0
 c. Undefined
 d. Undefined

136. _____ is the process in which two clone daughter cells are produced by the cell division of one bacterium.
 a. Bacteria growth0
 b. Thing
 c. Undefined
 d. Undefined

137. The _____ of an algebraic expression is the same equation, but without parentheses.
 a. Thing
 b. Expanded form0
 c. Undefined
 d. Undefined

138. In mathematics, _____ growth occurs when the growth rate of a function is always proportional to the function's current size.
 a. Exponential0
 b. Thing
 c. Undefined
 d. Undefined

139. _____ was a German mathematician and scientist of profound genius who contributed significantly to many fields, including number theory, analysis, differential geometry, geodesy, magnetism, astronomy, and optics.
 a. Karl Friedrich Gauss0
 b. Person
 c. Undefined
 d. Undefined

140. _____ are a measure of time.
 a. Thing
 b. Minutes0
 c. Undefined
 d. Undefined

141. The easiest _____ prime numbers resides in the use of the Sieve of Eratosthenes, an algorithm that discovers all prime numbers to a specified integer.
 a. Method for finding0
 b. Thing
 c. Undefined
 d. Undefined

Chapter 2. Equations and Inequalities in One Variable

1. A _____ is a symbolic representation denoting a quantity or expression. It often represents an "unknown" quantity that has the potential to change.
   - a. Thing
   - b. Variable0
   - c. Undefined
   - d. Undefined

2. The word _____ comes from the Latin word linearis, which means created by lines.
   - a. Linear0
   - b. Thing
   - c. Undefined
   - d. Undefined

3. A _____ is an equation in which each term is either a constant or the product of a constant times the first power of a variable.
   - a. Linear equation0
   - b. Thing
   - c. Undefined
   - d. Undefined

4. In mathematics and the mathematical sciences, a _____ is a fixed, but possibly unspecified, value. This is in contrast to a variable, which is not fixed.
   - a. Thing
   - b. Constant0
   - c. Undefined
   - d. Undefined

5. _____ is a fixed, but possibly unspecified, value. This is in contrast to a variable, which is not fixed.
   - a. Constant term0
   - b. Thing
   - c. Undefined
   - d. Undefined

6. A _____ is a set of possible values that a variable can take on in order to satisfy a given set of conditions, which may include equations and inequalities.
   - a. Solution set0
   - b. Thing
   - c. Undefined
   - d. Undefined

7. In common philosophical language, a proposition or _____, is the content of an assertion, that is, it is true-or-false and defined by the meaning of a particular piece of language.
   - a. Concept
   - b. Statement0
   - c. Undefined
   - d. Undefined

8. Equivalence is the condition of being _____ or essentially equal.
   - a. Thing
   - b. Equivalent0
   - c. Undefined
   - d. Undefined

9. Two mathematical objects are equal if and only if they are precisely the same in every way. This defines a binary relation, _____, denoted by the sign of _____ "=" in such a way that the statement "x = y" means that x and y are equal.
   - a. Thing
   - b. Equality0
   - c. Undefined
   - d. Undefined

10. _____ is a kind of property which exists as magnitude or multitude. It is among the basic classes of things along with quality, substance, change, and relation.

Chapter 2. Equations and Inequalities in One Variable

a. Thing
b. Amount0
c. Undefined
d. Undefined

11. An _____ is a combination of numbers, operators, grouping symbols and/or free variables and bound variables arranged in a meaningful way which can be evaluated..
a. Thing
b. Expression0
c. Undefined
d. Undefined

12. In mathematics, _____ is an elementary arithmetic operation. When one of the numbers is a whole number, _____ is the repeated sum of the other number.
a. Multiplication0
b. Thing
c. Undefined
d. Undefined

13. In mathematics, an _____ is a statement about the relative size or order of two objects.
a. Thing
b. Inequality0
c. Undefined
d. Undefined

14. In mathematics, the multiplicative inverse of a number x, denoted 1/x or x^{-1}, is the number which, when multiplied by x, yields 1. The multiplicative inverse of x is also called the _____ of x.
a. Reciprocal0
b. Thing
c. Undefined
d. Undefined

15. A _____ is a negotiable instrument instructing a financial institution to pay a specific amount of a specific currency from a specific demand account held in the maker/depositor's name with that institution. Both the maker and payee may be natural persons or legal entities.
a. Thing
b. Check0
c. Undefined
d. Undefined

16. A _____ is the part of a fraction that tells how many equal parts make up a whole, and which is used in the name of the fraction: "halves", "thirds", "fourths" or "quarters", "fifths" and so on.
a. Denominator0
b. Concept
c. Undefined
d. Undefined

17. In mathematics, and in particular in abstract algebra, the _____ is a property of binary operations that generalises the distributive law from elementary algebra.
a. Distributive property0
b. Thing
c. Undefined
d. Undefined

18. In arithmetic and algebra, when a number or expression is both preceded and followed by a binary operation, an _____ is required for which operation should be applied first.
a. Thing
b. Order of operations0
c. Undefined
d. Undefined

19. A _____ is a unit of length, usually used to measure distance, in a number of different systems, including Imperial units, United States customary units and Norwegian/Swedish mil. Its size can vary from system to system, but in each is between 1 and 10 kilometers. In contemporary English contexts _____ refers to either:

a. Thing b. Mile0
c. Undefined d. Undefined

20. In plane geometry, a _____ is a polygon with four equal sides, four right angles, and parallel opposite sides. In algebra, the _____ of a number is that number multiplied by itself.
   a. Thing b. Square0
   c. Undefined d. Undefined

21. In sociology and biology a _____ is the collection of people or organisms of a particular species living in a given geographic area or space, usually measured by a census.
   a. Population0 b. Thing
   c. Undefined d. Undefined

22. _____ is mass m per unit volume V.
   a. Thing b. Density0
   c. Undefined d. Undefined

23. In mathematics, a _____ is the result of multiplying, or an expression that identifies factors to be multiplied.
   a. Thing b. Product0
   c. Undefined d. Undefined

24. _____ is the process of reducing the number of significant digits in a number.
   a. Rounding0 b. Concept
   c. Undefined d. Undefined

25. In mathematics, a _____ number (or a _____) is a natural number that has exactly two (distinct) natural number divisors, which are 1 and the _____ number itself.
   a. Prime0 b. Thing
   c. Undefined d. Undefined

26. In mathematics, a _____ is an ordered list of objects. Like a set, it contains members, also called elements or terms, and the number of terms is called the length of the _____. Unlike a set, order matters, and the exact same elements can appear multiple times at different positions in the _____.
   a. Sequence0 b. Thing
   c. Undefined d. Undefined

27. Leonardo of Pisa (1170s or 1180s – 1250), also known as Leonardo Pisano, Leonardo Bonacci, Leonardo _____, or, most commonly, simply _____, was an Italian mathematician, considered by some "the most talented mathematician of the Middle Ages."
   a. Person b. Fibonacci0
   c. Undefined d. Undefined

28. _____ means in succession or back-to-back
   a. Consecutive0 b. Thing
   c. Undefined d. Undefined

Chapter 2. Equations and Inequalities in One Variable

29. A _____ is the sum of the elements of a sequence.
    a. Series0
    b. Thing
    c. Undefined
    d. Undefined

30. In geometry, a _____ is defined as a quadrilateral where all four of its angles are right angles.
    a. Thing
    b. Rectangle0
    c. Undefined
    d. Undefined

31. In classical geometry, a _____ of a circle or sphere is any line segment from its center to its boundary. By extension, the _____ of a circle or sphere is the length of any such segment. The _____ is half the diameter. In science and engineering the term _____ of curvature is commonly used as a synonym for _____.
    a. Thing
    b. Radius0
    c. Undefined
    d. Undefined

32. _____ is the application of tools and a processing medium to the transformation of raw materials into finished goods for sale.
    a. Manufacturing0
    b. Thing
    c. Undefined
    d. Undefined

33. A _____ is one of the basic shapes of geometry: a polygon with three vertices and three sides which are straight line segments.
    a. Thing
    b. Triangle0
    c. Undefined
    d. Undefined

34. In geometry, two lines or planes if one falls on the other in such a way as to create congruent adjacent angles. The term may be used as a noun or adjective. Thus, referring to Figure 1, the line AB is the _____ to CD through the point B.
    a. Perpendicular0
    b. Thing
    c. Undefined
    d. Undefined

35. In geometry, an _____ of a triangle is a straight line through a vertex and perpendicular to (i.e. forming a right angle with) the opposite side or an extension of the opposite side.
    a. Concept
    b. Altitude0
    c. Undefined
    d. Undefined

36. A _____ is a function that assigns a number to subsets of a given set.
    a. Thing
    b. Measure0
    c. Undefined
    d. Undefined

37. _____ is the distance around a given two-dimensional object. As a general rule, the _____ of a polygon can always be calculated by adding all the length of the sides together. So, the formula for triangles is P = a + b + c, where a, b and c stand for each side of it. For quadrilaterals the equation is P = a + b + c + d. For equilateral polygons, P = na, where n is the number of sides and a is the side length.
    a. Thing
    b. Perimeter0
    c. Undefined
    d. Undefined

38. The decimal separator is a symbol used to mark the boundary between the integral and the fractional parts of a decimal numeral. Terms implying the symbol used are _____ and decimal comma.
   a. Decimal point0
   b. Concept
   c. Undefined
   d. Undefined

39. _____ is a way of expressing a number as a fraction of 100 per cent meaning "per hundred".
   a. Percent0
   b. Thing
   c. Undefined
   d. Undefined

40. Deductive _____ is the kind of _____ in which the conclusion is necessitated by, or reached from, previously known facts (the premises).
   a. Reasoning0
   b. Thing
   c. Undefined
   d. Undefined

41. In mathematics, for a statement to be mathematically _____, such a statement must be true of all natural numbers.
   a. Thing
   b. Inductive0
   c. Undefined
   d. Undefined

42. Induction or _____, sometimes called inductive logic, is the process of reasoning in which the premises of an argument are believed to support the conclusion but do not ensure it.
   a. Inductive reasoning0
   b. Thing
   c. Undefined
   d. Undefined

43. Mathematical _____ is used to represent ideas.
   a. Notation0
   b. Thing
   c. Undefined
   d. Undefined

44. A _____ is a number, figure, or indicator that appears below the normal line of type, typically used in a formula, mathematical expression, or description of a chemical compound.
   a. Thing
   b. Subscript0
   c. Undefined
   d. Undefined

45. A _____ is a deliberate process for transforming one or more inputs into one or more results.
   a. Calculation0
   b. Thing
   c. Undefined
   d. Undefined

46. In _____ algebra, a *-ring is an associative ring with an antilinear, antiautomorphism * : A ¨ A which is an involution.
   a. Thing
   b. Star0
   c. Undefined
   d. Undefined

47. The act of _____ is the calculated approximation of a result which is usable even if input data may be incomplete, uncertain, or noisy.

Chapter 2. Equations and Inequalities in One Variable

    a. Estimating0
    b. Thing
    c. Undefined
    d. Undefined

48. The _____ of a solid object is the three-dimensional concept of how much space it occupies, often quantified numerically.
    a. Volume0
    b. Thing
    c. Undefined
    d. Undefined

49. In mathematics, a _____ is a quadric surface, with the following equation in Cartesian coordinates: $(x/a)^2 + (y/b)^2 = 1$.
    a. Thing
    b. Cylinder0
    c. Undefined
    d. Undefined

50. A _____ is the result of the addition of a set of numbers. The numbers may be natural numbers, complex numbers, matrices, or still more complicated objects. An infinite _____ is a subtle procedure known as a series.
    a. Thing
    b. Sum0
    c. Undefined
    d. Undefined

51. A _____ is a special kind of ratio, indicating a relationship between two measurements with different units, such as miles to gallons or cents to pounds.
    a. Rate0
    b. Thing
    c. Undefined
    d. Undefined

52. In mathematics, _____ are essentially word problems that are designed to use mathematical critical thinking in everyday situations.
    a. Thing
    b. Application problems0
    c. Undefined
    d. Undefined

53. _____ forms part of thinking. Considered the most complex of all intellectual functions, _____ has been defined as higher-order cognitive process that requires the modulation and control of more routine or fundamental skills.
    a. Thing
    b. Problem solving0
    c. Undefined
    d. Undefined

54. A _____ is a consumption tax charged at the point of purchase for certain goods and services.
    a. Sales tax0
    b. Thing
    c. Undefined
    d. Undefined

55. In geometry, an _____ is a point at which a line segment or ray terminates.
    a. Thing
    b. Endpoint0
    c. Undefined
    d. Undefined

56. In geometry and physics, _____ are half-lines that continue forever in one direction.
    a. Rays0
    b. Thing
    c. Undefined
    d. Undefined

Chapter 2. Equations and Inequalities in One Variable

57. In geometry, a _____ is a special kind of point, usually a corner of a polygon, polyhedron, or higher dimensional polytope. In the geometry of curves a _____ is a point of where the first derivative of curvature is zero. In graph theory, a _____ is the fundamental unit out of which graphs are formed
   a. Thing
   b. Vertex0
   c. Undefined
   d. Undefined

58. A _____ given two distinct points A and B on the _____, is the set of points C on the line containing points A and B such that A is not strictly between C and B.
   a. Thing
   b. Ray0
   c. Undefined
   d. Undefined

59. In mathematics, there are several meanings of _____ depending on the subject.
   a. Degree0
   b. Thing
   c. Undefined
   d. Undefined

60. A _____ is a movement of an object in a circular motion. A two-dimensional object rotates around a center (or point) of _____. A three-dimensional object rotates around a line called an axis. If the axis of _____ is within the body, the body is said to rotate upon itself, or spin—which implies relative speed and perhaps free-movement with angular momentum. A circular motion about an external point, e.g. the Earth about the Sun, is called an orbit or more properly an orbital revolution.
   a. Thing
   b. Rotation0
   c. Undefined
   d. Undefined

61. An angle equal to two right angles is called a _____ (equal to 180 degrees).
   a. Thing
   b. Straight angle0
   c. Undefined
   d. Undefined

62. In geometry and trigonometry, a _____ is defined as an angle between two straight intersecting lines of ninety degrees, or one-quarter of a circle.
   a. Right angle0
   b. Thing
   c. Undefined
   d. Undefined

63. Any angle larger than 90 degrees and less than 180 degrees, is called an _____ angle.
   a. Concept
   b. Obtuse0
   c. Undefined
   d. Undefined

64. Angles smaller than a right angle are called _____ angles (less than 90 degrees).
   a. Concept
   b. Acute0
   c. Undefined
   d. Undefined

65. A pair of angles is _____ if their respective measures sum to 180 degrees.
   a. Concept
   b. Supplementary0
   c. Undefined
   d. Undefined

66. In set theory and other branches of mathematics, two kinds of complements are defined, the relative _____ and the absolute _____.

Chapter 2. Equations and Inequalities in One Variable

a. Complement0
b. Thing
c. Undefined
d. Undefined

67. A pair of angles are _____ if the sum of their angles is 90°.
    a. Concept
    b. Complementary0
    c. Undefined
    d. Undefined

68. In mathematics, the additive inverse, or _____ of a number n is the number that, when added to n, yields zero. The additive inverse of n is denoted −n. For example, 7 is −7, because 7 + (−7) = 0, and the additive inverse of −0.3 is 0.3, because −0.3 + 0.3 = 0.
    a. Thing
    b. Opposite0
    c. Undefined
    d. Undefined

69. An _____ triange is a triangle with at least two sides of equal length.
    a. Thing
    b. Isosceles0
    c. Undefined
    d. Undefined

70. In mathematics, the _____ of a number n is the number that, when added to n, yields zero. The _____ of n is denoted −n. For example, 7 is −7, because 7 + (−7) = 0, and the _____ of −0.3 is 0.3, because −0.3 + 0.3 = 0.
    a. Thing
    b. Additive inverse0
    c. Undefined
    d. Undefined

71. In geometry, an _____ polygon is a polygon which has all sides of the same length.
    a. Thing
    b. Equilateral0
    c. Undefined
    d. Undefined

72. An _____ is a triangle in which all sides are of equal length.
    a. Equilateral triangle0
    b. Thing
    c. Undefined
    d. Undefined

73. An _____ is an angle formed by two sides of a simple polygon that share an endpoint, namely, the angle on the inner side of the polygon.
    a. Interior angle0
    b. Thing
    c. Undefined
    d. Undefined

74. _____ is the fee paid on borrowed money.
    a. Interest0
    b. Thing
    c. Undefined
    d. Undefined

75. _____ is a synonym for information.
    a. Thing
    b. Data0
    c. Undefined
    d. Undefined

76. In mathematics, the conjugate _____ or adjoint matrix of an m-by-n matrix A with complex entries is the n-by-m matrix A* obtained from A by taking the transpose and then taking the complex conjugate of each entry.

Chapter 2. Equations and Inequalities in One Variable

    a. Thing   b. Pairs0
    c. Undefined   d. Undefined

77. The _____ of measurement are a globally standardized and modernized form of the metric system.
    a. Thing   b. Units0
    c. Undefined   d. Undefined

78. In mathematics, a matrix can be thought of as each row or _____ being a vector. Hence, a space formed by row vectors or _____ vectors are said to be a row space or a _____ space.
    a. Concept   b. Column0
    c. Undefined   d. Undefined

79. The metre (or _____, see spelling differences) is a measure of length. It is the basic unit of length in the metric system and in the International System of Units (SI), used around the world for general and scientific purposes.
    a. Meter0   b. Concept
    c. Undefined   d. Undefined

80. _____ usually refers to money in the form of liquid currency, such as banknotes or coins.
    a. Cash0   b. Thing
    c. Undefined   d. Undefined

81. _____ is a form of periodic payment from an employer to an employee, which is specified in an employment contract.
    a. Gross pay0   b. Thing
    c. Undefined   d. Undefined

82. A _____ is a form of periodic payment from an employer to an employee, which is specified in an employment contract.
    a. Salary0   b. Thing
    c. Undefined   d. Undefined

83. A _____ is a compensation which workers receive in exchange for their labor.
    a. Thing   b. Wage0
    c. Undefined   d. Undefined

84. _____ is a membership organization owned by the 25,000+ financial institutions that issue its card
    a. Thing   b. MasterCard0
    c. Undefined   d. Undefined

85. A _____ is a system of payment named after the small plastic card issued to users of the system.
    a. Credit card0   b. Thing
    c. Undefined   d. Undefined

86. _____ mathematical functions take numeric arguments and produce numeric results.

Chapter 2. Equations and Inequalities in One Variable

    a. Miscellaneous0   b. Thing
    c. Undefined   d. Undefined

87. A _____ is a fee added to a customer's bill.
    a. Thing   b. Service charge0
    c. Undefined   d. Undefined

88. _____ of an object is its speed in a particular direction.
    a. Velocity0   b. Thing
    c. Undefined   d. Undefined

89. A _____ is a vehicle, missile or aircraft which obtains thrust by the reaction to the ejection of fast moving fluid from within a _____ engine.
    a. Rocket0   b. Thing
    c. Undefined   d. Undefined

90. In mathematics, a _____ may be described informally as a number that can be given by an infinite decimal representation.
    a. Real number0   b. Thing
    c. Undefined   d. Undefined

91. _____ is the state of being greater than any finite number, however large.
    a. Thing   b. Infinity0
    c. Undefined   d. Undefined

92. Mathematical _____ are the wide variety of ways to capture an abstract mathematical concept or relationship.
    a. Thing   b. Representations0
    c. Undefined   d. Undefined

93. In mathematics, an inequality is a statement about the relative size or order of two objects. For example 14 > 10, or 14 is _____ 10.
    a. Greater than0   b. Thing
    c. Undefined   d. Undefined

94. The _____, the average in everyday English, which is also called the arithmetic _____ (and is distinguished from the geometric _____ or harmonic _____). The average is also called the sample _____. The expected value of a random variable, which is also called the population _____.
    a. Thing   b. Mean0
    c. Undefined   d. Undefined

95. In elementary algebra, an _____ is a set that contains every real number between two indicated numbers and may contain the two numbers themselves.
    a. Thing   b. Interval0
    c. Undefined   d. Undefined

96. A _____ is a number that is less than zero.

a. Negative number0   b. Thing
c. Undefined   d. Undefined

97. _____ is the notation in which permitted values for a variable are expressed as ranging over a certain interval; "5 < x < 9" is an example of the application of _____.
a. Interval notation0   b. Thing
c. Undefined   d. Undefined

98. A _____ is a one-dimensional picture in which the integers are shown as specially-marked points evenly spaced on a line.
a. Thing   b. Number line0
c. Undefined   d. Undefined

99. In geometry, the _____ of an object is a point in some sense in the middle of the object.
a. Center0   b. Thing
c. Undefined   d. Undefined

100. _____ are objects, characters, or other concrete representations of ideas, concepts, or other abstractions.
a. Thing   b. Symbols0
c. Undefined   d. Undefined

101. In Euclidean geometry, a _____ is the set of all points in a plane at a fixed distance, called the radius, from a given point, the center.
a. Circle0   b. Thing
c. Undefined   d. Undefined

102. _____ interest refers to the fact that whenever interest is calculated, it is based not only on the original principal, but also on any unpaid interest that has been added to the principal.
a. Thing   b. Compound0
c. Undefined   d. Undefined

103. _____ is a temperature scale named after the German physicist Daniel Gabriel _____, who proposed it in 1724.
a. Thing   b. Fahrenheit0
c. Undefined   d. Undefined

104. _____ is, or relates to, the _____ temperature scale .
a. Celsius0   b. Thing
c. Undefined   d. Undefined

105. _____ is a physical property of a system that underlies the common notions of hot and cold; something that is hotter has the greater _____.
a. Temperature0   b. Thing
c. Undefined   d. Undefined

Chapter 2. Equations and Inequalities in One Variable

106. In Euclidean geometry, a uniform _____ is a linear transformation that enlargers or diminishes objects, and whose _____ factor is the same in all directions. This is also called homothethy.
   a. Thing
   b. Scale0
   c. Undefined
   d. Undefined

107. In mathematics, the _____ of a function is the set of all "output" values produced by that function. Given a function $f : A \to B$, the _____ of f, is defined to be the set $\{x \in B : x = f(a) \text{ for some } a \in A\}$.
   a. Thing
   b. Range0
   c. Undefined
   d. Undefined

108. In business, particularly accounting, a _____ is the time intervals that the accounts, statement, payments, or other calculations cover.
   a. Thing
   b. Period0
   c. Undefined
   d. Undefined

109. A _____ is a type of debt. All material things can be lent but this article focuses exclusively on monetary loans. Like all debt instruments, a _____ entails the redistribution of financial assets over time, between the lender and the borrower.
   a. Loan0
   b. Thing
   c. Undefined
   d. Undefined

110. _____ are a measure of time.
   a. Minutes0
   b. Thing
   c. Undefined
   d. Undefined

111. In mathematics, the _____ (or modulus) of a real number is its numerical value without regard to its sign.
   a. Absolute value0
   b. Thing
   c. Undefined
   d. Undefined

112. In mathematics and more specifically set theory, the _____ set is the unique set which contains no elements.
   a. Empty0
   b. Thing
   c. Undefined
   d. Undefined

113. _____, from Latin meaning "to make progress", is defined in two different ways. Pure economic _____ is the increase in wealth that an investor has from making an investment, taking into consideration all costs associated with that investment including the opportunity cost of capital.
   a. Thing
   b. Profit0
   c. Undefined
   d. Undefined

114. _____ are procedures that allow people to exchange information by one of several methods.
   a. Thing
   b. Communications0
   c. Undefined
   d. Undefined

115. In Euclidean geometry, a _____ is moving every point a constant distance in a specified direction.

a. Translation0 b. Concept
c. Undefined d. Undefined

116. The _____ integers are all the integers from zero on upwards.
a. Thing b. Nonnegative0
c. Undefined d. Undefined

117. _____ is a unit of speed, expressing the number of international miles covered per hour.
a. Thing b. Miles per hour0
c. Undefined d. Undefined

118. _____ is electromagnetic radiation with a wavelength that is visible to the eye (visible _____) or, in a technical or scientific context, electromagnetic radiation of any wavelength.
a. Thing b. Light0
c. Undefined d. Undefined

119. _____ is a mathematical science pertaining to the collection, analysis, interpretation or explanation, and presentation of data. It is applicable to a wide variety of academic disciplines, from the physical and social sciences to the humanities.
a. Thing b. Statistics0
c. Undefined d. Undefined

120. _____ is a branch of mathematics concerning the study of structure, relation and quantity.
a. Algebra0 b. Concept
c. Undefined d. Undefined

121. In mathematics, a _____ number is a number which can be expressed as a ratio of two integers. Non-integer _____ numbers (commonly called fractions) are usually written as the vulgar fraction a / b, where b is not zero.
a. Thing b. Rational0
c. Undefined d. Undefined

122. In mathematics, an _____ number is any real number that is not a rational number- that is, it is a number which cannot be expressed as a fraction m/n, where m and n are integers.
a. Irrational0 b. Thing
c. Undefined d. Undefined

123. In mathematics, an _____ is any real number that is not a rational number ¡ª that is, it is a number which cannot be expressed as m/n, where m and n are integers.
a. Thing b. Irrational number0
c. Undefined d. Undefined

124. In mathematics, _____ are any real number that is not a rational number ¡ª that is, it is a number which cannot be expressed as m/n, where m and n are integers.
a. Thing b. Irrational numbers0
c. Undefined d. Undefined

Chapter 3. Equations and Inequalities in Two Variables

1. _____ is a temperature scale named after the German physicist Daniel Gabriel _____ , who proposed it in 1724.
   a. Fahrenheit0
   b. Thing
   c. Undefined
   d. Undefined

2. _____ is, or relates to, the _____ temperature scale .
   a. Celsius0
   b. Thing
   c. Undefined
   d. Undefined

3. In mathematics, there are several meanings of _____ depending on the subject.
   a. Thing
   b. Degree0
   c. Undefined
   d. Undefined

4. _____ is a physical property of a system that underlies the common notions of hot and cold; something that is hotter has the greater _____.
   a. Thing
   b. Temperature0
   c. Undefined
   d. Undefined

5. Acid _____ ratio measures the ability of a company to use its near cash or quick assets to immediately extinguish its current liabilities.
   a. Test0
   b. Thing
   c. Undefined
   d. Undefined

6. In set theory and its applications throughout mathematics, _____ are a collection of sets (or sometimes other mathematical objects) that can be unambiguously defined by a property that all its members share.
   a. Thing
   b. Classes0
   c. Undefined
   d. Undefined

7. An _____ is a straight line around which a geometric figure can be rotated.
   a. Axis0
   b. Thing
   c. Undefined
   d. Undefined

8. In astronomy, geography, geometry and related sciences and contexts, a plane is said to be _____ at a given point if it is locally perpendicular to the gradient of the gravity field, i.e., with the direction of the gravitational force at that point.
   a. Thing
   b. Horizontal0
   c. Undefined
   d. Undefined

9. Mathematical _____ is used to represent ideas.
   a. Thing
   b. Notation0
   c. Undefined
   d. Undefined

10. _____ is a synonym for information.
    a. Data0
    b. Thing
    c. Undefined
    d. Undefined

11. _____ is the study of terms and their use — of words and compound words that are used in specific contexts.

Chapter 3. Equations and Inequalities in Two Variables

a. Terminology0
b. Thing
c. Undefined
d. Undefined

12. An _____ is a collection of two not necessarily distinct objects, one of which is distinguished as the first coordinate and the other as the second coordinate.
    a. Thing
    b. Ordered pair0
    c. Undefined
    d. Undefined

13. _____, either of the curved-bracket punctuation marks that together make a set of _____
    a. Parentheses0
    b. Thing
    c. Undefined
    d. Undefined

14. A _____ is a set of numbers that designate location in a given reference system, such as x,y in a planar _____ system or an x,y,z in a three-dimensional _____ system.
    a. Coordinate0
    b. Thing
    c. Undefined
    d. Undefined

15. In mathematics and its applications, a _____ is a system for assigning an n-tuple of numbers or scalars to each point in an n-dimensional space.
    a. Concept
    b. Coordinate system0
    c. Undefined
    d. Undefined

16. A _____ is a one-dimensional picture in which the integers are shown as specially-marked points evenly spaced on a line.
    a. Thing
    b. Number line0
    c. Undefined
    d. Undefined

17. In mathematics, a _____ may be described informally as a number that can be given by an infinite decimal representation.
    a. Real number0
    b. Thing
    c. Undefined
    d. Undefined

18. In geometry and trigonometry, a _____ is defined as an angle between two straight intersecting lines of ninety degrees, or one-quarter of a circle.
    a. Thing
    b. Right angle0
    c. Undefined
    d. Undefined

19. An _____ is when two lines intersect somewhere on a plane creating a right angle at intersection
    a. Thing
    b. Axes0
    c. Undefined
    d. Undefined

20. In mathematics, the _____ of a coordinate system is the point where the axes of the system intersect.
    a. Origin0
    b. Thing
    c. Undefined
    d. Undefined

21. A _____ consists of one quarter of the coordinate plane.

a. Quadrant0   b. Thing
c. Undefined   d. Undefined

22. The _____ of measurement are a globally standardized and modernized form of the metric system.
a. Units0   b. Thing
c. Undefined   d. Undefined

23. In mathematics, the conjugate _____ or adjoint matrix of an m-by-n matrix A with complex entries is the n-by-m matrix A* obtained from A by taking the transpose and then taking the complex conjugate of each entry.
a. Pairs0   b. Thing
c. Undefined   d. Undefined

24. _____ are external two-dimensional outlines, with the appearance or configuration of some thing - in contrast to the matter or content or substance of which it is composed.
a. Shapes0   b. Thing
c. Undefined   d. Undefined

25. In mathematics, the concept of a _____ tries to capture the intuitive idea of a geometrical one-dimensional and continuous object. A simple example is the circle.
a. Thing   b. Curve0
c. Undefined   d. Undefined

26. In mathematics, _____ are the intuitive idea of a geometrical one-dimensional and continuous object.
a. Thing   b. Curves0
c. Undefined   d. Undefined

27. _____ is a branch of mathematics concerning the study of structure, relation and quantity.
a. Concept   b. Algebra0
c. Undefined   d. Undefined

28. _____ over a given field is a polynomial with coefficients in that field.
a. Thing   b. Algebraic equation0
c. Undefined   d. Undefined

29. A _____ is a simplified and structured visual representation of concepts, ideas, constructions, relations, statistical data, anatomy etc used in all aspects of human activities to visualize and clarify the topic.
a. Diagram0   b. Thing
c. Undefined   d. Undefined

30. _____ means of or relating to the French philosopher and mathematician René Descartes.
a. Thing   b. Cartesian0
c. Undefined   d. Undefined

31. In mathematics, the _____ is used to determine each point uniquely in a plane through two numbers, usually called the x-coordinate and the y-coordinate of the point.

Chapter 3. Equations and Inequalities in Two Variables

a. Cartesian coordinate system0
b. Thing
c. Undefined
d. Undefined

32. _____ was a highly influential French philosopher, mathematician, scientist, and writer. Dubbed the "Founder of Modern Philosophy", and the "Father of Modern Mathematics". His theories provided the basis for the calculus of Newton and Leibniz, by applying infinitesimal calculus to the tangent line problem, thus permitting the evolution of that branch of modern mathematics

a. Person
b. Descartes0
c. Undefined
d. Undefined

33. In common philosophical language, a proposition or _____, is the content of an assertion, that is, it is true-or-false and defined by the meaning of a particular piece of language.

a. Statement0
b. Concept
c. Undefined
d. Undefined

34. A _____ is a symbolic representation denoting a quantity or expression. It often represents an "unknown" quantity that has the potential to change.

a. Thing
b. Variable0
c. Undefined
d. Undefined

35. The word _____ comes from the Latin word linearis, which means created by lines.

a. Thing
b. Linear0
c. Undefined
d. Undefined

36. A _____ is an equation in which each term is either a constant or the product of a constant times the first power of a variable.

a. Linear equation0
b. Thing
c. Undefined
d. Undefined

37. _____ is a notation for writing numbers that is often used by scientists and mathematicians to make it easier to write large and small numbers.

a. Scientific notation0
b. Thing
c. Undefined
d. Undefined

38. A _____ is a set of possible values that a variable can take on in order to satisfy a given set of conditions, which may include equations and inequalities.

a. Solution set0
b. Thing
c. Undefined
d. Undefined

39. _____ is the study of geometry using the principles of algebra. _____ can be explained more simply: it is concerned with defining geometrical shapes in a numerical way and extracting numerical information from that representation.

a. Thing
b. Analytic geometry0
c. Undefined
d. Undefined

40. Any point where a graph makes contact with an coordinate axis is called an _____ of the graph

Chapter 3. Equations and Inequalities in Two Variables

a. Intercept0
b. Thing
c. Undefined
d. Undefined

41. In mathematics, an _____ is a statement about the relative size or order of two objects.
    a. Inequality0
    b. Thing
    c. Undefined
    d. Undefined

42. The _____ is the y- coordinate of a point within a two dimensional coordinate system. It is sometimes used to refer to the axis rather than the distance along the coordinate system.
    a. Ordinate0
    b. Thing
    c. Undefined
    d. Undefined

43. _____ are the basic objects of study in graph theory. Informally speaking, a graph is a set of objects called points, nodes, or vertices connected by links called lines or edges.
    a. Graphs0
    b. Thing
    c. Undefined
    d. Undefined

44. In linear algebra, the _____ of an n-by-n square matrix A is defined to be the sum of the elements on the main diagonal of A,
    a. Trace0
    b. Thing
    c. Undefined
    d. Undefined

45. The mathematical concept of a _____ expresses the intuitive idea of deterministic dependence between two quantities, one of which is viewed as primary and the other as secondary. A _____ then is a way to associate a unique output for each input of a specified type, for example, a real number or an element of a given set.
    a. Function0
    b. Thing
    c. Undefined
    d. Undefined

46. In geographic information systems, a _____ comprises an entity with a geographic location, typically determined by points, arcs, or polygons. Carriageways and cadastres exemplify _____ data.
    a. Thing
    b. Feature0
    c. Undefined
    d. Undefined

47. A _____ of a number is the product of that number with any integer.
    a. Thing
    b. Multiple0
    c. Undefined
    d. Undefined

48. In mathematics, the _____ of a function is the set of all "output" values produced by that function. Given a function $f : A \to B$, the _____ of f, is defined to be the set $\{x \in B : x = f(a)$ for some $a \in A\}$.
    a. Range0
    b. Thing
    c. Undefined
    d. Undefined

49. A _____ is a special kind of ratio, indicating a relationship between two measurements with different units, such as miles to gallons or cents to pounds.

Chapter 3. Equations and Inequalities in Two Variables

a. Rate0
b. Thing
c. Undefined
d. Undefined

50. In mathematics and the mathematical sciences, a _____ is a fixed, but possibly unspecified, value. This is in contrast to a variable, which is not fixed.
    a. Thing
    b. Constant0
    c. Undefined
    d. Undefined

51. The _____ rule, also known as a slipstick, is a mechanical analog computer, consisting of at least two finely divided scales , most often a fixed outer pair and a movable inner one, with a sliding window called the cursor.
    a. Thing
    b. Slide0
    c. Undefined
    d. Undefined

52. A _____ is a negotiable instrument instructing a financial institution to pay a specific amount of a specific currency from a specific demand account held in the maker/depositor's name with that institution. Both the maker and payee may be natural persons or legal entities.
    a. Check0
    b. Thing
    c. Undefined
    d. Undefined

53. The _____ (symbol _____) and the millibar (symbol mbar, also mb) are units of pressure.
    a. Bar0
    b. Thing
    c. Undefined
    d. Undefined

54. _____ are rectangular tables (or grids) of information, often financial information.
    a. Spreadsheets0
    b. Thing
    c. Undefined
    d. Undefined

55. _____ is often used to describe the measurement of the steepness, incline, gradient, or grade of a straight line. The _____ is defined as the ratio of the "rise" divided by the "run" between two points on a line, or in other words, the ratio of the altitude change to the horizontal distance between any two points on the line.
    a. Slope0
    b. Thing
    c. Undefined
    d. Undefined

56. A _____ is a quantity that denotes the proportional amount or magnitude of one quantity relative to another.
    a. Thing
    b. Ratio0
    c. Undefined
    d. Undefined

57. A _____ is an abstract model that uses mathematical language to describe the behavior of a system. Eykhoff defined a _____ as 'a representation of the essential aspects of an existing system which presents knowledge of that system in usable form'.
    a. Mathematical model0
    b. Thing
    c. Undefined
    d. Undefined

58. The _____, the average in everyday English, which is also called the arithmetic _____ (and is distinguished from the geometric _____ or harmonic _____). The average is also called the sample _____. The expected value of a random variable, which is also called the population _____.

Chapter 3. Equations and Inequalities in Two Variables

a. Mean0
b. Thing
c. Undefined
d. Undefined

59. A _____ is a function that assigns a number to subsets of a given set.
a. Thing
b. Measure0
c. Undefined
d. Undefined

60. A _____ is a numeral used to indicate a count. The most common use of the word today is to name the part of a fraction that tells the number or count of equal parts.
a. Numerator0
b. Thing
c. Undefined
d. Undefined

61. In mathematics, the additive inverse, or _____ of a number n is the number that, when added to n, yields zero. The additive inverse of n is denoted −n. For example, 7 is −7, because 7 + (−7) = 0, and the additive inverse of −0.3 is 0.3, because −0.3 + 0.3 = 0.
a. Thing
b. Opposite0
c. Undefined
d. Undefined

62. A _____ is the part of a fraction that tells how many equal parts make up a whole, and which is used in the name of the fraction: "halves", "thirds", "fourths" or "quarters", "fifths" and so on.
a. Concept
b. Denominator0
c. Undefined
d. Undefined

63. In mathematics, the _____ of a number n is the number that, when added to n, yields zero. The _____ of n is denoted −n. For example, 7 is −7, because 7 + (−7) = 0, and the _____ of −0.3 is 0.3, because −0.3 + 0.3 = 0.
a. Additive inverse0
b. Thing
c. Undefined
d. Undefined

64. In mathematics, defined and _____ are used to explain whether or not expressions have meaningful, sensible, and unambiguous values.
a. Thing
b. Undefined0
c. Undefined
d. Undefined

65. An _____ is a combination of numbers, operators, grouping symbols and/or free variables and bound variables arranged in a meaningful way which can be evaluated..
a. Expression0
b. Thing
c. Undefined
d. Undefined

66. In geometry, two lines or planes if one falls on the other in such a way as to create congruent adjacent angles. The term may be used as a noun or adjective. Thus, referring to Figure 1, the line AB is the _____ to CD through the point B.
a. Thing
b. Perpendicular0
c. Undefined
d. Undefined

67. In mathematics, a _____ is a two-dimensional manifold or surface that is perfectly flat.

Chapter 3. Equations and Inequalities in Two Variables

    a. Plane0   b. Thing
    c. Undefined   d. Undefined

68. In mathematics, a _____ is the result of multiplying, or an expression that identifies factors to be multiplied.
    a. Thing   b. Product0
    c. Undefined   d. Undefined

69. In mathematics, the multiplicative inverse of a number x, denoted $1/x$ or x^{-1}, is the number which, when multiplied by x, yields 1. The multiplicative inverse of x is also called the _____ of x.
    a. Reciprocal0   b. Thing
    c. Undefined   d. Undefined

70. In mathematics, a _____ is a demonstration that, assuming certain axioms, some statement is necessarily true.
    a. Proof0   b. Thing
    c. Undefined   d. Undefined

71. _____ are objects, characters, or other concrete representations of ideas, concepts, or other abstractions.
    a. Thing   b. Symbols0
    c. Undefined   d. Undefined

72. A _____ is a unit of length, usually used to measure distance, in a number of different systems, including Imperial units, United States customary units and Norwegian/Swedish mil. Its size can vary from system to system, but in each is between 1 and 10 kilometers. In contemporary English contexts _____ refers to either:
    a. Mile0   b. Thing
    c. Undefined   d. Undefined

73. _____, from Latin meaning "to make progress", is defined in two different ways. Pure economic _____ is the increase in wealth that an investor has from making an investment, taking into consideration all costs associated with that investment including the opportunity cost of capital.
    a. Thing   b. Profit0
    c. Undefined   d. Undefined

74. _____ is a kind of property which exists as magnitude or multitude. It is among the basic classes of things along with quality, substance, change, and relation.
    a. Thing   b. Amount0
    c. Undefined   d. Undefined

75. In geometry, a line _____ is a part of a line that is bounded by two end points, and contains every point on the line between its end points.
    a. Concept   b. Segment0
    c. Undefined   d. Undefined

76. A _____ is a part of a line that is bounded by two end points, and contains every point on the line between its end points.

Chapter 3. Equations and Inequalities in Two Variables 37

    a. Thing
    c. Undefined
    b. Line segment0
    d. Undefined

77. The _____ are the only integral domain whose positive elements are well-ordered, and in which order is preserved by addition. Like the natural numbers, the _____ form a countably infinite set. The set of all _____ is usually denoted in mathematics by a boldface Z .
    a. Thing
    c. Undefined
    b. Integers0
    d. Undefined

78. The plus and _____ signs are mathematical symbols used to represent the notions of positive and negative as well as the operations of addition and subtraction.
    a. Minus0
    c. Undefined
    b. Thing
    d. Undefined

79. A _____ is one of the basic shapes of geometry: a polygon with three vertices and three sides which are straight line segments.
    a. Triangle0
    c. Undefined
    b. Thing
    d. Undefined

80. _____ usually refers to money in the form of liquid currency, such as banknotes or coins.
    a. Cash0
    c. Undefined
    b. Thing
    d. Undefined

81. An _____ triange is a triangle with at least two sides of equal length.
    a. Isosceles0
    c. Undefined
    b. Thing
    d. Undefined

82. A _____ is a consumption tax charged at the point of purchase for certain goods and services.
    a. Thing
    c. Undefined
    b. Sales tax0
    d. Undefined

83. In combinatorial mathematics, a _____ is an un-ordered collection of unique elements.
    a. Combination0
    c. Undefined
    b. Concept
    d. Undefined

84. In mathematics, _____ geometry was the traditional name for the geometry of three-dimensional Euclidean space — for practical purposes the kind of space we live in.
    a. Solid0
    c. Undefined
    b. Thing
    d. Undefined

85. In mathematics, a matrix can be thought of as each row or _____ being a vector. Hence, a space formed by row vectors or _____ vectors are said to be a row space or a _____ space.
    a. Concept
    c. Undefined
    b. Column0
    d. Undefined

86. In geometry, a _____ is defined as a quadrilateral where all four of its angles are right angles.

a. Thing
b. Rectangle0
c. Undefined
d. Undefined

87. U.S. liquid _____ is legally defined as 231 cubic inches, and is equal to 3.785411784 litres or abotu 0.13368 cubic feet. This is the most common definition of a _____. The U.S. fluid ounce is defined as 1/128 of a U.S. _____.
   a. Thing
   b. Gallon0
   c. Undefined
   d. Undefined

88. A _____ is the result of the addition of a set of numbers. The numbers may be natural numbers, complex numbers, matrices, or still more complicated objects. An infinite _____ is a subtle procedure known as a series.
   a. Sum0
   b. Thing
   c. Undefined
   d. Undefined

89. _____ is a form of periodic payment from an employer to an employee, which is specified in an employment contract.
   a. Gross pay0
   b. Thing
   c. Undefined
   d. Undefined

90. A _____ is a type of debt. All material things can be lent but this article focuses exclusively on monetary loans. Like all debt instruments, a _____ entails the redistribution of financial assets over time, between the lender and the borrower.
   a. Loan0
   b. Thing
   c. Undefined
   d. Undefined

91. A _____ is a form of periodic payment from an employer to an employee, which is specified in an employment contract.
   a. Salary0
   b. Thing
   c. Undefined
   d. Undefined

92. In statistics, a _____ measure is one which is measuring what is supposed to measure.
   a. Valid0
   b. Thing
   c. Undefined
   d. Undefined

93. In mathematics, a _____ of a k-place relation $L \subseteq X_1 \times ... \times X_k$ is one of the sets X_j, $1 \leq j \leq k$. In the special case where k = 2 and $L \subseteq X_1 \times X_2$ is a function $L : X_1 \to X_2$, it is conventional to refer to X_1 as the _____ of the function and to refer to X_2 as the codomain of the function.
   a. Domain0
   b. Thing
   c. Undefined
   d. Undefined

94. An _____ or member of a set is an object that when collected together make up the set.
   a. Thing
   b. Element0
   c. Undefined
   d. Undefined

95. In mathematics, the _____ , or members of a set or more generally a class are all those objects which when collected together make up the set or class.

Chapter 3. Equations and Inequalities in Two Variables

a. Thing
b. Elements0
c. Undefined
d. Undefined

96. _____ is a test to determine if a relation or its graph is a function or not
a. Thing
b. Vertical line test0
c. Undefined
d. Undefined

97. In mathematics, the _____ f is the collection of all ordered pairs . In particular, graph means the graphical representation of this collection, in the form of a curve or surface, together with axes, etc. Graphing on a Cartesian plane is sometimes referred to as curve sketching.
a. Graph of a function0
b. Thing
c. Undefined
d. Undefined

98. In economics _____ means before deductions brutto, e.g. _____ domestic or national product, or _____ profit or income
a. Gross0
b. Thing
c. Undefined
d. Undefined

99. _____ is an adjective usually refering to being in the centre.
a. Thing
b. Central0
c. Undefined
d. Undefined

100. In plane geometry, a _____ is a polygon with four equal sides, four right angles, and parallel opposite sides. In algebra, the _____ of a number is that number multiplied by itself.
a. Square0
b. Thing
c. Undefined
d. Undefined

101. _____ is electromagnetic radiation with a wavelength that is visible to the eye (visible _____) or, in a technical or scientific context, electromagnetic radiation of any wavelength.
a. Thing
b. Light0
c. Undefined
d. Undefined

102. In Euclidean geometry, a _____ is the set of all points in a plane at a fixed distance, called the radius, from a given point, the center.
a. Thing
b. Circle0
c. Undefined
d. Undefined

103. In classical geometry, a _____ of a circle or sphere is any line segment from its center to its boundary. By extension, the _____ of a circle or sphere is the length of any such segment. The _____ is half the diameter. In science and engineering the term _____ of curvature is commonly used as a synonym for _____.
a. Radius0
b. Thing
c. Undefined
d. Undefined

Chapter 3. Equations and Inequalities in Two Variables

104. _____ is the distance around a given two-dimensional object. As a general rule, the _____ of a polygon can always be calculated by adding all the length of the sides together. So, the formula for triangles is P = a + b + c, where a, b and c stand for each side of it. For quadrilaterals the equation is P = a + b + c + d. For equilateral polygons, P = na, where n is the number of sides and a is the side length.
   a. Perimeter0
   b. Thing
   c. Undefined
   d. Undefined

105. In mathematics, an _____ is any of the arguments, i.e. "inputs", to a function. Thus if we have a function f(x), then x is a _____.
   a. Independent variable0
   b. Thing
   c. Undefined
   d. Undefined

106. In a function the _____, is the variable which is the value, i.e. the "output", of the function.
   a. Thing
   b. Dependent variable0
   c. Undefined
   d. Undefined

107. Equivalence is the condition of being _____ or essentially equal.
   a. Thing
   b. Equivalent0
   c. Undefined
   d. Undefined

108. A _____, is a symbolized depiction of space which highlights relations between components of that space. Most usually a _____ is a two-dimensional, geometrically accurate representation of a three-dimensional space.
   a. Thing
   b. Map0
   c. Undefined
   d. Undefined

109. In mathematics, an _____, mean, or central tendency of a data set refers to a measure of the "middle" or "expected" value of the data set.
   a. Average0
   b. Concept
   c. Undefined
   d. Undefined

110. _____ is a unit of speed, expressing the number of international miles covered per hour.
   a. Miles per hour0
   b. Thing
   c. Undefined
   d. Undefined

111. _____ are a measure of time.
   a. Thing
   b. Minutes0
   c. Undefined
   d. Undefined

112. _____ or investing is a term with several closely-related meanings in business management, finance and economics, related to saving or deferring consumption.
   a. Investment0
   b. Thing
   c. Undefined
   d. Undefined

113. In mathematics, a _____ is the set of all points in three-dimensional space (R^3) which are at distance r from a fixed point of that space, where r is a positive real number called the radius of the _____. The fixed point is called the center or centre, and is not part of the _____ itself.

Chapter 3. Equations and Inequalities in Two Variables

a. Sphere0
b. Thing
c. Undefined
d. Undefined

114. The _____ is the distance around a closed curve. _____ is a kind of perimeter.
   a. Thing
   b. Circumference0
   c. Undefined
   d. Undefined

115. The _____ of a solid object is the three-dimensional concept of how much space it occupies, often quantified numerically.
   a. Thing
   b. Volume0
   c. Undefined
   d. Undefined

116. In mathematics, a _____ can mean either an element of the set {1, 2, 3, ...} (i.e the positive integers) or an element of the set {0, 1, 2, 3, ...} (i.e. the non-negative integers).
   a. Concept
   b. Whole number0
   c. Undefined
   d. Undefined

117. _____ is a term used in accounting, economics and finance with reference to the fact that assets with finite lives lose value over time.
   a. Depreciation0
   b. Thing
   c. Undefined
   d. Undefined

118. A function on the real numbers is called a _____ if it can be written as a finite linear combination of indicator functions of half-open intervals.
   a. Thing
   b. Step function0
   c. Undefined
   d. Undefined

119. _____ element of an element x with respect to a binary operation * with identity element e is an element y such that x * y = y * x = e. In particular,
   a. Thing
   b. Inverse0
   c. Undefined
   d. Undefined

120. In mathematics and logic, a _____ proof is a way of showing the truth or falsehood of a given statement by a straightforward combination of established facts, usually existing lemmas and theorems, without making any further assumptions.
   a. Thing
   b. Direct0
   c. Undefined
   d. Undefined

121. _____ is the relationship between two variables, like a ratio in which the two quantities being compared are different units.
   a. Thing
   b. Direct variation0
   c. Undefined
   d. Undefined

122. _____, Greek for "knowledge of nature," is the branch of science concerned with the discovery and characterization of universal laws which govern matter, energy, space, and time.

a. Thing
b. Physics0
c. Undefined
d. Undefined

123. In mathematics, two quantities are called _____ if they vary in such a way that one of the quantities is a constant multiple of the other, or equivalently if they have a constant ratio.
   a. Proportional0
   b. Thing
   c. Undefined
   d. Undefined

124. _____ is a special mathematical relationship between two quantities. Two quantities are called proportional if they vary in such a way that one of the quantities is a constant multiple of the other, or equivalently if they have a constant ratio.
   a. Thing
   b. Proportionality0
   c. Undefined
   d. Undefined

125. A _____ is a three-dimensional solid object bounded by six square faces, facets, or sides, with three meeting at each vertex.
   a. Cube0
   b. Thing
   c. Undefined
   d. Undefined

126. In mathematics, a _____ of a number x is a number r such that $r^2 = x$, or in words, a number r whose square (the result of multiplying the number by itself) is x.
   a. Square root0
   b. Thing
   c. Undefined
   d. Undefined

127. In mathematics, a _____ of a complex-valued function f is a member x of the domain of f such that f(x) vanishes at x, that is, x : f (x) = 0.
   a. Thing
   b. Root0
   c. Undefined
   d. Undefined

128. _____ of an object is its speed in a particular direction.
   a. Velocity0
   b. Thing
   c. Undefined
   d. Undefined

129. A _____ of a number is a number a such that $a^3 = x$.
   a. Thing
   b. Cube root0
   c. Undefined
   d. Undefined

130. In the scientific method, an _____ (Latin: ex-+-periri, "of (or from) trying"), is a set of actions and observations, performed in the context of solving a particular problem or question, in order to support or falsify a hypothesis or research concerning phenomena.
   a. Experiment0
   b. Thing
   c. Undefined
   d. Undefined

131. _____ is a relationship among three or more variables in which each pair of variables varies directly or inversely.

Chapter 3. Equations and Inequalities in Two Variables

    a. Joint variation0
    b. Thing
    c. Undefined
    d. Undefined

132. In geometry, a _____ (Greek words diairo = divide and metro = measure) of a circle is any straight line segment that passes through the centre and whose endpoints are on the circular boundary, or, in more modern usage, the length of such a line segment. When using the word in the more modern sense, one speaks of the _____ rather than a _____, because all diameters of a circle have the same length. This length is twice the radius. The _____ of a circle is also the longest chord that the circle has.
    a. Diameter0
    b. Thing
    c. Undefined
    d. Undefined

133. In physics, _____ is an influence that may cause an object to accelerate. It may be experienced as a lift, a push, or a pull. The actual acceleration of the body is determined by the vector sum of all forces acting on it, known as net _____ or resultant _____.
    a. Thing
    b. Force0
    c. Undefined
    d. Undefined

134. In statistics the _____ of an event i is the number n_i of times the event occurred in the experiment or the study. These frequencies are often graphically represented in histograms.
    a. Concept
    b. Frequency0
    c. Undefined
    d. Undefined

135. In mathematics, a _____ is a quadric surface, with the following equation in Cartesian coordinates: $(x/_a)^2 + (y/_b)^2 = 1$.
    a. Cylinder0
    b. Thing
    c. Undefined
    d. Undefined

136. _____ is the ability to hold, receive or absorb, or a measure thereof, similar to the concept of volume.
    a. Concept
    b. Capacity0
    c. Undefined
    d. Undefined

137. A _____ is an object that is attached to a pivot point so that it can swing freely.
    a. Thing
    b. Pendulum0
    c. Undefined
    d. Undefined

138. In business, particularly accounting, a _____ is the time intervals that the accounts, statement, payments, or other calculations cover.
    a. Thing
    b. Period0
    c. Undefined
    d. Undefined

139. Multiple Signal Classification, also known as _____, is an algorithm used for frequency estimation and emitter location.
    a. Music0
    b. Thing
    c. Undefined
    d. Undefined

Chapter 3. Equations and Inequalities in Two Variables

140. The metre (or _____, see spelling differences) is a measure of length. It is the basic unit of length in the metric system and in the International System of Units (SI), used around the world for general and scientific purposes.
   a. Meter0
   b. Concept
   c. Undefined
   d. Undefined

141. Sir Isaac _____, was an English physicist, mathematician, astronomer, natural philosopher, and alchemist, regarded by many as the greatest figure in the history of science
   a. Newton0
   b. Person
   c. Undefined
   d. Undefined

142. _____ algebra (sometimes called General algebra) is the field of mathematics that studies the ideas common to all algebraic structures.
   a. Universal0
   b. Thing
   c. Undefined
   d. Undefined

143. The _____ is defined as the summation of all particles and energy that exist and the space-time which all events occur.
   a. Thing
   b. Universe0
   c. Undefined
   d. Undefined

144. Sir _____ was an English physicist, mathematician, astronomer, natural philosopher, and alchemist, regarded by many as the greatest figure in the history of science.
   a. Person
   b. Isaac Newton0
   c. Undefined
   d. Undefined

145. _____ is the property of a physical object that quantifies the amount of matter and energy it is equivalent to.
   a. Thing
   b. Mass0
   c. Undefined
   d. Undefined

146. _____ is mass m per unit volume V.
   a. Density0
   b. Thing
   c. Undefined
   d. Undefined

147. A _____ signifies a point or points of probability on a subject e.g., the _____ of creativity, which allows for the formation of rule or norm or law by interpretation of the phenomena events that can be created.
   a. Thing
   b. Principle0
   c. Undefined
   d. Undefined

148. In geometry, the _____ of an object is a point in some sense in the middle of the object.
   a. Thing
   b. Center0
   c. Undefined
   d. Undefined

149. The existence and properties of _____ are the basis of Euclid's parallel postulate. _____ are two lines on the same plane that do not intersect even assuming that lines extend to infinity in either direction.

Chapter 3. Equations and Inequalities in Two Variables

a. Parallel lines0
b. Thing
c. Undefined
d. Undefined

150. _____ is a reaction force applied by a stretched string on the objects which stretch it.
   a. Thing
   b. Tension0
   c. Undefined
   d. Undefined

151. In mathematics, a _____ is an ordered list of objects. Like a set, it contains members, also called elements or terms, and the number of terms is called the length of the _____. Unlike a set, order matters, and the exact same elements can appear multiple times at different positions in the _____.
   a. Sequence0
   b. Thing
   c. Undefined
   d. Undefined

152. _____ or arithmetics is the oldest and most elementary branch of mathematics, used by almost everyone, for tasks ranging from simple daily counting to advanced science and business calculations.
   a. Arithmetic0
   b. Thing
   c. Undefined
   d. Undefined

153. Blaise _____ was a French mathematician, physicist, and religious philosopher.
   a. Person
   b. Pascal0
   c. Undefined
   d. Undefined

154. _____ was a French mathematician, physicist, and religious philosopher.
   a. Person
   b. Blaise Pascal0
   c. Undefined
   d. Undefined

Chapter 4. Systems of Linear Equations and Inequalities

1. Acid _____ ratio measures the ability of a company to use its near cash or quick assets to immediately extinguish its current liabilities.
   a. Test0
   b. Thing
   c. Undefined
   d. Undefined

2. A _____ is a symbolic representation denoting a quantity or expression. It often represents an "unknown" quantity that has the potential to change.
   a. Thing
   b. Variable0
   c. Undefined
   d. Undefined

3. The word _____ comes from the Latin word linearis, which means created by lines.
   a. Linear0
   b. Thing
   c. Undefined
   d. Undefined

4. A _____ is an equation in which each term is either a constant or the product of a constant times the first power of a variable.
   a. Thing
   b. Linear equation0
   c. Undefined
   d. Undefined

5. A _____ is a set of possible values that a variable can take on in order to satisfy a given set of conditions, which may include equations and inequalities.
   a. Solution set0
   b. Thing
   c. Undefined
   d. Undefined

6. An _____ is a collection of two not necessarily distinct objects, one of which is distinguished as the first coordinate and the other as the second coordinate.
   a. Thing
   b. Ordered pair0
   c. Undefined
   d. Undefined

7. In mathematics, the conjugate _____ or adjoint matrix of an m-by-n matrix A with complex entries is the n-by-m matrix A* obtained from A by taking the transpose and then taking the complex conjugate of each entry.
   a. Thing
   b. Pairs0
   c. Undefined
   d. Undefined

8. An _____ is when two lines intersect somewhere on a plane creating a right angle at intersection
   a. Thing
   b. Axes0
   c. Undefined
   d. Undefined

9. _____ are the basic objects of study in graph theory. Informally speaking, a graph is a set of objects called points, nodes, or vertices connected by links called lines or edges.
   a. Graphs0
   b. Thing
   c. Undefined
   d. Undefined

10. _____ are a set of equations containing multiple variables.
    a. Systems of equations0
    b. Thing
    c. Undefined
    d. Undefined

Chapter 4. Systems of Linear Equations and Inequalities

11. _____, either of the curved-bracket punctuation marks that together make a set of _____
    a. Thing
    b. Parentheses0
    c. Undefined
    d. Undefined

12. A _____ is a set of numbers that designate location in a given reference system, such as x,y in a planar _____ system or an x,y,z in a three-dimensional _____ system.
    a. Coordinate0
    b. Thing
    c. Undefined
    d. Undefined

13. In mathematics and more specifically set theory, the _____ set is the unique set which contains no elements.
    a. Empty0
    b. Thing
    c. Undefined
    d. Undefined

14. The _____ are the only integral domain whose positive elements are well-ordered, and in which order is preserved by addition. Like the natural numbers, the _____ form a countably infinite set. The set of all _____ is usually denoted in mathematics by a boldface Z .
    a. Integers0
    b. Thing
    c. Undefined
    d. Undefined

15. In mathematics, the _____ of two sets A and B is the set that contains all elements of A that also belong to B (or equivalently, all elements of B that also belong to A), but no other elements.
    a. Thing
    b. Intersection0
    c. Undefined
    d. Undefined

16. In mathematics, a _____ is a constant multiplicative factor of a certain object. The object can be such things as a variable, a vector, a function, etc. For example, the _____ of $9x^2$ is 9.
    a. Thing
    b. Coefficient0
    c. Undefined
    d. Undefined

17. In mathematics, the additive inverse, or _____ of a number n is the number that, when added to n, yields zero. The additive inverse of n is denoted −n. For example, 7 is −7, because 7 + (−7) = 0, and the additive inverse of −0.3 is 0.3, because −0.3 + 0.3 = 0.
    a. Opposite0
    b. Thing
    c. Undefined
    d. Undefined

18. A _____ is a negotiable instrument instructing a financial institution to pay a specific amount of a specific currency from a specific demand account held in the maker/depositor's name with that institution. Both the maker and payee may be natural persons or legal entities.
    a. Check0
    b. Thing
    c. Undefined
    d. Undefined

19. In common philosophical language, a proposition or _____, is the content of an assertion, that is, it is true-or-false and defined by the meaning of a particular piece of language.
    a. Statement0
    b. Concept
    c. Undefined
    d. Undefined

Chapter 4. Systems of Linear Equations and Inequalities

20. _____ or arithmetics is the oldest and most elementary branch of mathematics, used by almost everyone, for tasks ranging from simple daily counting to advanced science and business calculations.
    a. Arithmetic0
    b. Thing
    c. Undefined
    d. Undefined

21. In mathematics, an _____ is a statement about the relative size or order of two objects.
    a. Thing
    b. Inequality0
    c. Undefined
    d. Undefined

22. In mathematics, _____ is an elementary arithmetic operation. When one of the numbers is a whole number, _____ is the repeated sum of the other number.
    a. Thing
    b. Multiplication0
    c. Undefined
    d. Undefined

23. Two mathematical objects are equal if and only if they are precisely the same in every way. This defines a binary relation, _____, denoted by the sign of _____ "=" in such a way that the statement "x = y" means that x and y are equal.
    a. Thing
    b. Equality0
    c. Undefined
    d. Undefined

24. A _____ of a number is the product of that number with any integer.
    a. Thing
    b. Multiple0
    c. Undefined
    d. Undefined

25. _____ is the state of being greater than any finite real or natural number, however large.
    a. Infinite0
    b. Thing
    c. Undefined
    d. Undefined

26. The _____ is used to discard one of the variables in an equation, only to replace it with the actual value when solving multiple equations.
    a. Substitution method0
    b. Thing
    c. Undefined
    d. Undefined

27. An _____ is a combination of numbers, operators, grouping symbols and/or free variables and bound variables arranged in a meaningful way which can be evaluated..
    a. Expression0
    b. Thing
    c. Undefined
    d. Undefined

28. In sociology and biology a _____ is the collection of people or organisms of a particular species living in a given geographic area or space, usually measured by a census.
    a. Population0
    b. Thing
    c. Undefined
    d. Undefined

29. In mathematics, a _____ is an n-tuple with n being 3.

Chapter 4. Systems of Linear Equations and Inequalities

    a. Triple0
    c. Undefined
    b. Thing
    d. Undefined

30. In mathematics, a _____ is a two-dimensional manifold or surface that is perfectly flat.
    a. Plane0
    b. Thing
    c. Undefined
    d. Undefined

31. In mathematics, _____ are two-dimensional manifolds or surfaces that are perfectly flat.
    a. Thing
    b. Planes0
    c. Undefined
    d. Undefined

32. In mathematics and its applications, a _____ is a system for assigning an n-tuple of numbers or scalars to each point in an n-dimensional space.
    a. Coordinate system0
    b. Concept
    c. Undefined
    d. Undefined

33. In geometry, two lines or planes if one falls on the other in such a way as to create congruent adjacent angles. The term may be used as a noun or adjective. Thus, referring to Figure 1, the line AB is the _____ to CD through the point B.
    a. Thing
    b. Perpendicular0
    c. Undefined
    d. Undefined

34. _____ is a set, with some particular properties and usually some additional structure, such as the operations of addition or multiplication, for instance.
    a. Space0
    b. Thing
    c. Undefined
    d. Undefined

35. In finance, a _____ is collateral that the holder of a position in securities, options, or futures contracts has to deposit to cover the credit risk of his counterparty.
    a. Margin0
    b. Thing
    c. Undefined
    d. Undefined

36. In physics, a _____ may refer to the scalar _____ or to the vector _____.
    a. Thing
    b. Potential0
    c. Undefined
    d. Undefined

37. A _____ is a simplified and structured visual representation of concepts, ideas, constructions, relations, statistical data, anatomy etc used in all aspects of human activities to visualize and clarify the topic.
    a. Thing
    b. Diagram0
    c. Undefined
    d. Undefined

38. A _____ is a unit of length, usually used to measure distance, in a number of different systems, including Imperial units, United States customary units and Norwegian/Swedish mil. Its size can vary from system to system, but in each is between 1 and 10 kilometers. In contemporary English contexts _____ refers to either:
    a. Thing
    b. Mile0
    c. Undefined
    d. Undefined

Chapter 4. Systems of Linear Equations and Inequalities

39. In algebra, a _____ is a function depending on *n* that associates a scalar, det(A), to every *n*×*n* square matrix *A*.
   a. Determinant0
   b. Thing
   c. Undefined
   d. Undefined

40. In plane geometry, a _____ is a polygon with four equal sides, four right angles, and parallel opposite sides. In algebra, the _____ of a number is that number multiplied by itself.
   a. Thing
   b. Square0
   c. Undefined
   d. Undefined

41. In computer science an _____ is a data structure that consists of a group of elements having a single name that are accessed by indexing. In most programming languages each element has the same data type and the _____ occupies a continuous area of storage.
   a. Array0
   b. Thing
   c. Undefined
   d. Undefined

42. A _____ is 360° or 2δ radians.
   a. Turn0
   b. Thing
   c. Undefined
   d. Undefined

43. An _____ of a product of sums expresses it as a sum of products by using the fact that multiplication distributes over addition.
   a. Expansion0
   b. Thing
   c. Undefined
   d. Undefined

44. In mathematics, a _____ is the result of multiplying, or an expression that identifies factors to be multiplied.
   a. Thing
   b. Product0
   c. Undefined
   d. Undefined

45. In mathematics, a matrix can be thought of as each row or _____ being a vector. Hence, a space formed by row vectors or _____ vectors are said to be a row space or a _____ space.
   a. Concept
   b. Column0
   c. Undefined
   d. Undefined

46. A _____ can refer to a line joining two nonadjacent vertices of a polygon or polyhedron, or in some contexts any upward or downward sloping line. .
   a. Thing
   b. Diagonal0
   c. Undefined
   d. Undefined

47. A _____ decimal is a number whose decimal representation eventually becomes periodic (i.e. the same number sequence _____ indefinitely).
   a. Thing
   b. Repeating0
   c. Undefined
   d. Undefined

48. In linear algebra, a _____ of a matrix A is the determinant of some smaller square matrix, cut down from A.

Chapter 4. Systems of Linear Equations and Inequalities 51

    a. Thing
    c. Undefined
    b. Minor0
    d. Undefined

49. An _____ or member of a set is an object that when collected together make up the set.
    a. Element0
    c. Undefined
    b. Thing
    d. Undefined

50. In mathematics, the _____ , or members of a set or more generally a class are all those objects which when collected together make up the set or class.
    a. Thing
    c. Undefined
    b. Elements0
    d. Undefined

51. The plus and _____ signs are mathematical symbols used to represent the notions of positive and negative as well as the operations of addition and subtraction.
    a. Thing
    c. Undefined
    b. Minus0
    d. Undefined

52. _____ was a German mathematician and philosopher. He invented calculus independently of Newton, and his notation is the one in general use since.
    a. Person
    c. Undefined
    b. Leibniz0
    d. Undefined

53. In mathematics, the _____ is two monic polynomials P and Q over a field k.
    a. Resultant0
    c. Undefined
    b. Thing
    d. Undefined

54. _____ was a French mathematician and astronomer who put the final capstone on mathematical astronomy by summarizing and extending the work of his predecessors in his five volume Mécanique Céleste. This masterpiece translated the geometrical study of classical mechanics used by Isaac Newton to one based on calculus, known as physical mechanics.
    a. Pierre Laplace0
    c. Undefined
    b. Person
    d. Undefined

55. In mathematics and the mathematical sciences, a _____ is a fixed, but possibly unspecified, value. This is in contrast to a variable, which is not fixed.
    a. Thing
    c. Undefined
    b. Constant0
    d. Undefined

56. _____ is a fixed, but possibly unspecified, value. This is in contrast to a variable, which is not fixed.
    a. Thing
    c. Undefined
    b. Constant term0
    d. Undefined

57. Mathematical _____ is used to represent ideas.
    a. Thing
    c. Undefined
    b. Notation0
    d. Undefined

Chapter 4. Systems of Linear Equations and Inequalities

58. _____ is the transport of people on a trip/journey or the process or time involved in a person or object moving from one location to another.
   a. Travel0
   b. Thing
   c. Undefined
   d. Undefined

59. Leonhard _____ was a pioneering Swiss mathematician and physicist, who spent most of his life in Russia and Germany.
   a. Euler0
   b. Person
   c. Undefined
   d. Undefined

60. _____ is a kind of property which exists as magnitude or multitude. It is among the basic classes of things along with quality, substance, change, and relation.
   a. Thing
   b. Amount0
   c. Undefined
   d. Undefined

61. Fixed costs are expenses whose total does not change in proportion to the activity of a business.Unit fixed costs decline with volume following a retangular hyperbola as the volume of production.Variable costs by contrast change in relation to the activity of a business such as sales or production volume.Along with variable costs,fixed costs make up one of the two components of total cost. In the most simple production function total cost is equal to fixed costs plus variable costs.In accounting terminology, fixed costs will broadly include all costs which are not included in cost of goods sold, and variable costs are those captured in costs of goods sold. The implicit assumption required to make the equivalence between the accounting and economics terminology is that the accounting period is equal to the period in which fixed costs do not vary in relation to production. In practice, this equivalence does not always hold and depending on the period under consideration by management, some overhead expenses can be adjusted by management, and the specific allocation of each expense to each category will be decided under cost accounting.In business planning and management accounting, usage of the terms fixed costs, variable costs and others will often differ from usage in economics, and may depend on the intended use. For example, costs may be segregated into per unit costs fixed costs per period, and variable costs as a proportion of revenue. Capital expenditures will usually be allocated separately, and depending on the purpose, a portion may be regularly allocated to expenses as depreciation and amortization and seen as a _____ per period, or the entire amount may be considered upfront fixed costs.
   a. Fixed cost0
   b. Thing
   c. Undefined
   d. Undefined

62. _____ are expenses whose total does not change in proportion to the activity of a business, within the relevant time period or scale of production
   a. Thing
   b. Fixed costs0
   c. Undefined
   d. Undefined

63. _____ forms part of thinking. Considered the most complex of all intellectual functions, _____ has been defined as higher-order cognitive process that requires the modulation and control of more routine or fundamental skills.
   a. Thing
   b. Problem solving0
   c. Undefined
   d. Undefined

64. Regrouping is the act of putting ones into groups of 10. For example, the 1 on the far right of 131 would be denoted _____ if the digit of the number being subtracted is larger than 1, such as 131-99.

Chapter 4. Systems of Linear Equations and Inequalities

a. By 100
b. Thing
c. Undefined
d. Undefined

65. _____ or investing is a term with several closely-related meanings in business management, finance and economics, related to saving or deferring consumption.
a. Investment0
b. Thing
c. Undefined
d. Undefined

66. _____ is the fee paid on borrowed money.
a. Interest0
b. Thing
c. Undefined
d. Undefined

67. U.S. liquid _____ is legally defined as 231 cubic inches, and is equal to 3.785411784 litres or abotu 0.13368 cubic feet. This is the most common definition of a _____. The U.S. fluid ounce is defined as 1/128 of a U.S. _____.
a. Thing
b. Gallon0
c. Undefined
d. Undefined

68. Equivalence is the condition of being _____ or essentially equal.
a. Thing
b. Equivalent0
c. Undefined
d. Undefined

69. Initial objects are also called _____, and terminal objects are also called final.
a. Thing
b. Coterminal0
c. Undefined
d. Undefined

70. A _____ is a special kind of ratio, indicating a relationship between two measurements with different units, such as miles to gallons or cents to pounds.
a. Rate0
b. Thing
c. Undefined
d. Undefined

71. In mathematics, an _____, mean, or central tendency of a data set refers to a measure of the "middle" or "expected" value of the data set.
a. Concept
b. Average0
c. Undefined
d. Undefined

72. _____ is a unit of speed, expressing the number of international miles covered per hour.
a. Thing
b. Miles per hour0
c. Undefined
d. Undefined

73. _____ is a temperature scale named after the German physicist Daniel Gabriel _____ , who proposed it in 1724.
a. Thing
b. Fahrenheit0
c. Undefined
d. Undefined

74. _____ is, or relates to, the _____ temperature scale .

54 *Chapter 4. Systems of Linear Equations and Inequalities*

    a. Celsius0   b. Thing
    c. Undefined   d. Undefined

75. _____ is a physical property of a system that underlies the common notions of hot and cold; something that is hotter has the greater _____.
    a. Thing   b. Temperature0
    c. Undefined   d. Undefined

76. In Euclidean geometry, a uniform _____ is a linear transformation that enlargers or diminishes objects, and whose _____ factor is the same in all directions. This is also called homothethy.
    a. Scale0   b. Thing
    c. Undefined   d. Undefined

77. A _____ is the result of the addition of a set of numbers. The numbers may be natural numbers, complex numbers, matrices, or still more complicated objects. An infinite _____ is a subtle procedure known as a series.
    a. Sum0   b. Thing
    c. Undefined   d. Undefined

78. In chemistry, a _____ is substance made by combining two or more different materials in such a way that no chemical reaction occurs.
    a. Thing   b. Mixture0
    c. Undefined   d. Undefined

79. _____ usually refers to money in the form of liquid currency, such as banknotes or coins.
    a. Cash0   b. Thing
    c. Undefined   d. Undefined

80. _____ is the application of tools and a processing medium to the transformation of raw materials into finished goods for sale.
    a. Manufacturing0   b. Thing
    c. Undefined   d. Undefined

81. In economics, supply and _____ describe market relations between prospective sellers and buyers of a good.
    a. Demand0   b. Thing
    c. Undefined   d. Undefined

82. _____ is a synonym for information.
    a. Thing   b. Data0
    c. Undefined   d. Undefined

83. In finance and economics, _____ is the process of finding the present value of an amount of cash at some future date, and along with compounding cash forms the basis of time value of money calculations.
    a. Thing   b. Discount0
    c. Undefined   d. Undefined

Chapter 4. Systems of Linear Equations and Inequalities

84. In mathematics, a _____ function in the sense of algebraic geometry is an everywhere-defined, polynomial function on an algebraic variety V with values in the field K over which V is defined.
   a. Thing
   b. Regular0
   c. Undefined
   d. Undefined

85. An _____ is a straight line around which a geometric figure can be rotated.
   a. Thing
   b. Axis0
   c. Undefined
   d. Undefined

86. In astronomy, geography, geometry and related sciences and contexts, a plane is said to be _____ at a given point if it is locally perpendicular to the gradient of the gravity field, i.e., with the direction of the gravitational force at that point.
   a. Thing
   b. Horizontal0
   c. Undefined
   d. Undefined

87. In mathematics, _____ geometry was the traditional name for the geometry of three-dimensional Euclidean space — for practical purposes the kind of space we live in.
   a. Thing
   b. Solid0
   c. Undefined
   d. Undefined

88. _____ is often used to describe the measurement of the steepness, incline, gradient, or grade of a straight line. The _____ is defined as the ratio of the "rise" divided by the "run" between two points on a line, or in other words, the ratio of the altitude change to the horizontal distance between any two points on the line.
   a. Thing
   b. Slope0
   c. Undefined
   d. Undefined

89. In elementary algebra, an _____ is a set that contains every real number between two indicated numbers and may contain the two numbers themselves.
   a. Thing
   b. Interval0
   c. Undefined
   d. Undefined

90. In mathematics, an inequality is a statement about the relative size or order of two objects. For example 14 > 10, or 14 is _____ 10.
   a. Thing
   b. Greater than0
   c. Undefined
   d. Undefined

91. _____ is the notation in which permitted values for a variable are expressed as ranging over a certain interval; "5 < x < 9" is an example of the application of _____.
   a. Thing
   b. Interval notation0
   c. Undefined
   d. Undefined

92. In mathematics, the multiplicative inverse of a number x, denoted $1/x$ or x^{-1}, is the number which, when multiplied by x, yields 1. The multiplicative inverse of x is also called the _____ of x.
   a. Thing
   b. Reciprocal0
   c. Undefined
   d. Undefined

Chapter 4. Systems of Linear Equations and Inequalities

93. In mathematics, the _____ of a number n is the number that, when added to n, yields zero. The _____ of n is denoted −n. For example, 7 is −7, because 7 + (−7) = 0, and the _____ of −0.3 is 0.3, because −0.3 + 0.3 = 0.
    a. Thing
    b. Additive inverse0
    c. Undefined
    d. Undefined

94. In mathematics, an _____ number is any real number that is not a rational number- that is, it is a number which cannot be expressed as a fraction m/n, where m and n are integers.
    a. Irrational0
    b. Thing
    c. Undefined
    d. Undefined

95. In mathematics, an _____ is any real number that is not a rational number ¡ª that is, it is a number which cannot be expressed as m/n, where m and n are integers.
    a. Irrational number0
    b. Thing
    c. Undefined
    d. Undefined

96. In mathematics, _____ are any real number that is not a rational number ¡ª that is, it is a number which cannot be expressed as m/n, where m and n are integers.
    a. Thing
    b. Irrational numbers0
    c. Undefined
    d. Undefined

97. In mathematics, the _____ f is the collection of all ordered pairs . In particular, graph means the graphical representation of this collection, in the form of a curve or surface, together with axes, etc. Graphing on a Cartesian plane is sometimes referred to as curve sketching.
    a. Graph of a function0
    b. Thing
    c. Undefined
    d. Undefined

98. The mathematical concept of a _____ expresses the intuitive idea of deterministic dependence between two quantities, one of which is viewed as primary and the other as secondary. A _____ then is a way to associate a unique output for each input of a specified type, for example, a real number or an element of a given set.
    a. Function0
    b. Thing
    c. Undefined
    d. Undefined

99. A _____ is one of the basic shapes of geometry: a polygon with three vertices and three sides which are straight line segments.
    a. Triangle0
    b. Thing
    c. Undefined
    d. Undefined

100. In mathematics, there are several meanings of _____ depending on the subject.
    a. Thing
    b. Degree0
    c. Undefined
    d. Undefined

101. _____ is a business term for the amount of money that a company receives from its activities in a given period, mostly from sales of products and/or services to customers
    a. Thing
    b. Revenue0
    c. Undefined
    d. Undefined

Chapter 4. Systems of Linear Equations and Inequalities

102. _____, from Latin meaning "to make progress", is defined in two different ways. Pure economic _____ is the increase in wealth that an investor has from making an investment, taking into consideration all costs associated with that investment including the opportunity cost of capital.
  a. Profit0
  b. Thing
  c. Undefined
  d. Undefined

103. _____ was an Greek philosopher. He is best known for a theorem in trigonometry that bears his name.
  a. Pythagoras0
  b. Person
  c. Undefined
  d. Undefined

104. _____ was a pre-Socratic Greek philosopher of southern Italy and a member of the Eleatic School founded by Parmenides.
  a. Person
  b. Zeno of Elea0
  c. Undefined
  d. Undefined

105. Deductive _____ is the kind of _____ in which the conclusion is necessitated by, or reached from, previously known facts (the premises).
  a. Reasoning0
  b. Thing
  c. Undefined
  d. Undefined

106. _____ are a set of problems devised by Zeno of Elea to support Parmenides' doctrine that "all is one" and that, contrary to the evidence of our senses, the belief in plurality and change is mistaken, and in particular that motion is nothing but an illusion.
  a. Thing
  b. Zeno's paradoxes0
  c. Undefined
  d. Undefined

Chapter 5. Exponents and Polynomials

1. Acid _____ ratio measures the ability of a company to use its near cash or quick assets to immediately extinguish its current liabilities.
   - a. Thing
   - b. Test0
   - c. Undefined
   - d. Undefined

2. Equivalence is the condition of being _____ or essentially equal.
   - a. Thing
   - b. Equivalent0
   - c. Undefined
   - d. Undefined

3. An _____ is a combination of numbers, operators, grouping symbols and/or free variables and bound variables arranged in a meaningful way which can be evaluated..
   - a. Expression0
   - b. Thing
   - c. Undefined
   - d. Undefined

4. A _____ is a symbolic representation denoting a quantity or expression. It often represents an "unknown" quantity that has the potential to change.
   - a. Thing
   - b. Variable0
   - c. Undefined
   - d. Undefined

5. _____ is a branch of mathematics concerning the study of structure, relation and quantity.
   - a. Algebra0
   - b. Concept
   - c. Undefined
   - d. Undefined

6. In mathematics, _____ expressions is used to reduce the expression into the lowest possible term.
   - a. Simplifying0
   - b. Thing
   - c. Undefined
   - d. Undefined

7. A _____ is a three-dimensional solid object bounded by six square faces, facets, or sides, with three meeting at each vertex.
   - a. Cube0
   - b. Thing
   - c. Undefined
   - d. Undefined

8. In plane geometry, a _____ is a polygon with four equal sides, four right angles, and parallel opposite sides. In algebra, the _____ of a number is that number multiplied by itself.
   - a. Square0
   - b. Thing
   - c. Undefined
   - d. Undefined

9. _____ is a mathematical operation, written a^n, involving two numbers, the base a and the exponent n.
   - a. Thing
   - b. Exponentiating0
   - c. Undefined
   - d. Undefined

10. _____ is a mathematical operation, written a^n, involving two numbers, the base a and the exponent n.
    - a. Exponentiation0
    - b. Thing
    - c. Undefined
    - d. Undefined

11. The _____ of a solid object is the three-dimensional concept of how much space it occupies, often quantified numerically.

a. Thing
b. Volume0
c. Undefined
d. Undefined

12. _____ has many meanings, most of which simply .
a. Thing
b. Power0
c. Undefined
d. Undefined

13. In mathematics, a _____ may be described informally as a number that can be given by an infinite decimal representation.
a. Thing
b. Real number0
c. Undefined
d. Undefined

14. The _____ are the only integral domain whose positive elements are well-ordered, and in which order is preserved by addition. Like the natural numbers, the _____ form a countably infinite set. The set of all _____ is usually denoted in mathematics by a boldface Z .
a. Thing
b. Integers0
c. Undefined
d. Undefined

15. In mathematics, a _____ is the result of multiplying, or an expression that identifies factors to be multiplied.
a. Product0
b. Thing
c. Undefined
d. Undefined

16. In mathematics, a _____ is an expression that is constructed from one or more variables and constants, using only the operations of addition, subtraction, multiplication, and constant positive whole number exponents. is a _____. Note in particular that division by an expression containing a variable is not in general allowed in polynomials. [1]
a. Thing
b. Polynomial0
c. Undefined
d. Undefined

17. In mathematics, _____ is an elementary arithmetic operation. When one of the numbers is a whole number, _____ is the repeated sum of the other number.
a. Thing
b. Multiplication0
c. Undefined
d. Undefined

18. In mathematics, a _____ is the end result of a division problem. It can also be expressed as the number of times the divisor divides into the dividend.
a. Quotient0
b. Thing
c. Undefined
d. Undefined

19. In common philosophical language, a proposition or _____, is the content of an assertion, that is, it is true-or-false and defined by the meaning of a particular piece of language.
a. Concept
b. Statement0
c. Undefined
d. Undefined

20. In mathematics, a _____ is a demonstration that, assuming certain axioms, some statement is necessarily true.

a. Proof0
b. Thing
c. Undefined
d. Undefined

21. In mathematics, factorization (British English: factorisation) or factoring is the decomposition of an object (for example, a number, a polynomial, or a matrix) into a product of other objects, or _____, which when multiplied together give the original.
   a. Factors0
   b. Thing
   c. Undefined
   d. Undefined

22. Mathematical _____ is used to represent ideas.
   a. Notation0
   b. Thing
   c. Undefined
   d. Undefined

23. _____ is a notation for writing numbers that is often used by scientists and mathematicians to make it easier to write large and small numbers.
   a. Thing
   b. Scientific notation0
   c. Undefined
   d. Undefined

24. The decimal separator is a symbol used to mark the boundary between the integral and the fractional parts of a decimal numeral. Terms implying the symbol used are _____ and decimal comma.
   a. Concept
   b. Decimal point0
   c. Undefined
   d. Undefined

25. In mathematics, an inequality is a statement about the relative size or order of two objects. For example 14 > 10, or 14 is _____ 10.
   a. Greater than0
   b. Thing
   c. Undefined
   d. Undefined

26. The _____ of an algebraic expression is the same equation, but without parentheses.
   a. Thing
   b. Expanded form0
   c. Undefined
   d. Undefined

27. _____ or arithmetics is the oldest and most elementary branch of mathematics, used by almost everyone, for tasks ranging from simple daily counting to advanced science and business calculations.
   a. Arithmetic0
   b. Thing
   c. Undefined
   d. Undefined

28. A _____ is 360° or 2δ radians.
   a. Thing
   b. Turn0
   c. Undefined
   d. Undefined

29. _____ is a synonym for information.
   a. Data0
   b. Thing
   c. Undefined
   d. Undefined

Chapter 5. Exponents and Polynomials 61

30. _____, or tropical cyclones are meterological terms for a storm system characterized by a low pressure center and thunderstorms that produces strong wind and flooding rain.
   a. Thing
   b. Hurricanes0
   c. Undefined
   d. Undefined

31. In business, particularly accounting, a _____ is the time intervals that the accounts, statement, payments, or other calculations cover.
   a. Period0
   b. Thing
   c. Undefined
   d. Undefined

32. A _____ is a quantity that denotes the proportional amount or magnitude of one quantity relative to another.
   a. Ratio0
   b. Thing
   c. Undefined
   d. Undefined

33. In _____ algebra, a *-ring is an associative ring with an antilinear, antiautomorphism * : A ¨ A which is an involution.
   a. Star0
   b. Thing
   c. Undefined
   d. Undefined

34. _____ is the transport of people on a trip/journey or the process or time involved in a person or object moving from one location to another.
   a. Thing
   b. Travel0
   c. Undefined
   d. Undefined

35. _____ is a set, with some particular properties and usually some additional structure, such as the operations of addition or multiplication, for instance.
   a. Thing
   b. Space0
   c. Undefined
   d. Undefined

36. _____ is electromagnetic radiation with a wavelength that is visible to the eye (visible _____) or, in a technical or scientific context, electromagnetic radiation of any wavelength.
   a. Light0
   b. Thing
   c. Undefined
   d. Undefined

37. A _____ or lightyear is a unit of measurement of length, specifically the distance light travels in a vacuum in one year.
   a. Light year0
   b. Thing
   c. Undefined
   d. Undefined

38. A _____ is a unit of length, usually used to measure distance, in a number of different systems, including Imperial units, United States customary units and Norwegian/Swedish mil. Its size can vary from system to system, but in each is between 1 and 10 kilometers. In contemporary English contexts _____ refers to either:
   a. Thing
   b. Mile0
   c. Undefined
   d. Undefined

39. A _____ is a system of payment named after the small plastic card issued to users of the system.

a. Thing
c. Undefined
b. Credit card0
d. Undefined

40. The _____ or kilogramme is the SI base unit of mass. It is defined as being equal to the mass of the international prototype of the _____.
   a. Thing
   c. Undefined
   b. Kilogram0
   d. Undefined

41. _____ is the property of a physical object that quantifies the amount of matter and energy it is equivalent to.
   a. Mass0
   c. Undefined
   b. Thing
   d. Undefined

42. The _____ is used to discard one of the variables in an equation, only to replace it with the actual value when solving multiple equations.
   a. Substitution method0
   c. Undefined
   b. Thing
   d. Undefined

43. A _____ is the result of the addition of a set of numbers. The numbers may be natural numbers, complex numbers, matrices, or still more complicated objects. An infinite _____ is a subtle procedure known as a series.
   a. Sum0
   c. Undefined
   b. Thing
   d. Undefined

44. _____ is a business term for the amount of money that a company receives from its activities in a given period, mostly from sales of products and/or services to customers
   a. Revenue0
   c. Undefined
   b. Thing
   d. Undefined

45. In mathematics, a _____ is a particular kind of polynomial, having just one term.
   a. Thing
   c. Undefined
   b. Monomial0
   d. Undefined

46. In mathematics and the mathematical sciences, a _____ is a fixed, but possibly unspecified, value. This is in contrast to a variable, which is not fixed.
   a. Constant0
   c. Undefined
   b. Thing
   d. Undefined

47. In mathematics, a set is called _____ if there is a bijection between the set and some set of the form {1, 2, ..., n} where n is a natural number.
   a. Finite0
   c. Undefined
   b. Thing
   d. Undefined

48. In elementary algebra, a _____ is a polynomial with two terms: the sum of two monomials. It is the simplest kind of polynomial except for a monomial.
   a. Binomial0
   c. Undefined
   b. Thing
   d. Undefined

Chapter 5. Exponents and Polynomials

49. A _____ is a polynomial consisting of three terms; in other words, it is the sum of three monomials.
    a. Thing
    b. Trinomial0
    c. Undefined
    d. Undefined

50. In mathematics, there are several meanings of _____ depending on the subject.
    a. Thing
    b. Degree0
    c. Undefined
    d. Undefined

51. The _____ is the maximum of the degrees of all terms in the polynomial.
    a. Degree of a polynomial0
    b. Thing
    c. Undefined
    d. Undefined

52. In mathematics, a _____ is a constant multiplicative factor of a certain object. The object can be such things as a variable, a vector, a function, etc. For example, the _____ of $9x^2$ is 9.
    a. Coefficient0
    b. Thing
    c. Undefined
    d. Undefined

53. In mathematics, a matrix can be thought of as each row or _____ being a vector. Hence, a space formed by row vectors or _____ vectors are said to be a row space or a _____ space.
    a. Concept
    b. Column0
    c. Undefined
    d. Undefined

54. In mathematics, and in particular in abstract algebra, the _____ is a property of binary operations that generalises the distributive law from elementary algebra.
    a. Thing
    b. Distributive property0
    c. Undefined
    d. Undefined

55. In mathematics, the additive inverse, or _____ of a number n is the number that, when added to n, yields zero. The additive inverse of n is denoted −n. For example, 7 is −7, because 7 + (−7) = 0, and the additive inverse of −0.3 is 0.3, because −0.3 + 0.3 = 0.
    a. Opposite0
    b. Thing
    c. Undefined
    d. Undefined

56. _____, either of the curved-bracket punctuation marks that together make a set of _____
    a. Thing
    b. Parentheses0
    c. Undefined
    d. Undefined

57. In mathematics, the _____ of a number n is the number that, when added to n, yields zero. The _____ of n is denoted −n. For example, 7 is −7, because 7 + (−7) = 0, and the _____ of −0.3 is 0.3, because −0.3 + 0.3 = 0.
    a. Thing
    b. Additive inverse0
    c. Undefined
    d. Undefined

58. _____ is a kind of property which exists as magnitude or multitude. It is among the basic classes of things along with quality, substance, change, and relation.

Chapter 5. Exponents and Polynomials

    a. Amount0   b. Thing
    c. Undefined   d. Undefined

59. _____, from Latin meaning "to make progress", is defined in two different ways. Pure economic _____ is the increase in wealth that an investor has from making an investment, taking into consideration all costs associated with that investment including the opportunity cost of capital.
    a. Thing   b. Profit0
    c. Undefined   d. Undefined

60. The mathematical concept of a _____ expresses the intuitive idea of deterministic dependence between two quantities, one of which is viewed as primary and the other as secondary. A _____ then is a way to associate a unique output for each input of a specified type, for example, a real number or an element of a given set.
    a. Function0   b. Thing
    c. Undefined   d. Undefined

61. _____ of an object is its speed in a particular direction.
    a. Thing   b. Velocity0
    c. Undefined   d. Undefined

62. The _____, the average in everyday English, which is also called the arithmetic _____ (and is distinguished from the geometric _____ or harmonic _____). The average is also called the sample _____. The expected value of a random variable, which is also called the population _____.
    a. Mean0   b. Thing
    c. Undefined   d. Undefined

63. In mathematics, a _____ can mean either an element of the set {1, 2, 3, ...} (i.e the positive integers) or an element of the set {0, 1, 2, 3, ...} (i.e. the non-negative integers).
    a. Concept   b. Whole number0
    c. Undefined   d. Undefined

64. In mathematics the _____ refers to the identity: $a^2 - b^2 = (a+b)(a-b)$
    a. Thing   b. Difference of two squares0
    c. Undefined   d. Undefined

65. _____ also sometimes known as the double distributive property or more colloquially as foiling, is commonly taught to US high school students learning algebra as a mnemonic for remembering how to multiply two binomials polynomials with two terms.
    a. FOIL method0   b. Thing
    c. Undefined   d. Undefined

66. The _____ is commonly taught to US high school students learning algebra as a mnemonic for remembering how to multiply two binomials.
    a. FOIL rule0   b. Thing
    c. Undefined   d. Undefined

Chapter 5. Exponents and Polynomials

67. A _____ is a special kind of ratio, indicating a relationship between two measurements with different units, such as miles to gallons or cents to pounds.
    a. Thing
    b. Rate0
    c. Undefined
    d. Undefined

68. _____ is the fee paid on borrowed money.
    a. Thing
    b. Interest0
    c. Undefined
    d. Undefined

69. An _____ is the fee paid on borrow money.
    a. Concept
    b. Interest rate0
    c. Undefined
    d. Undefined

70. In mathematics, the _____ divisor of two non-zero integers, is the largest positive integer that divides both numbers without remainder.
    a. Greatest common0
    b. Thing
    c. Undefined
    d. Undefined

71. In Math the greates common divisor sometimes known as the _____ of two non- zero integers.
    a. Thing
    b. Greatest common factor0
    c. Undefined
    d. Undefined

72. In abstract algebra, _____ consists of sets with binary operations that satisfy certain axioms.
    a. Grouping0
    b. Thing
    c. Undefined
    d. Undefined

73. _____ is the largest positive integer that divides both numbers without remainder.
    a. Common Factor0
    b. Thing
    c. Undefined
    d. Undefined

74. In mathematics, _____ is the decomposition of an object into a product of other objects, or factors, which when multiplied together give the original.
    a. Thing
    b. Factoring0
    c. Undefined
    d. Undefined

75. _____ is the application of tools and a processing medium to the transformation of raw materials into finished goods for sale.
    a. Thing
    b. Manufacturing0
    c. Undefined
    d. Undefined

76. In mathematics, the _____ (or modulus) of a real number is its numerical value without regard to its sign.
    a. Absolute value0
    b. Thing
    c. Undefined
    d. Undefined

77. A _____ are accounts maintained by commercial banks, savings and loan associations, credit unions, and mutual savings banks that pay interest but can not be used directly as money by, for example, writing a cheque.

a. Thing
b. Savings account0
c. Undefined
d. Undefined

78. In algebra, a _____ is a function depending on n that associates a scalar, det(A), to every $n \times n$ square matrix A.
a. Determinant0
b. Thing
c. Undefined
d. Undefined

79. _____ is a fixed, but possibly unspecified, value. This is in contrast to a variable, which is not fixed.
a. Thing
b. Constant term0
c. Undefined
d. Undefined

80. In mathematics, a _____ of an integer n, also called a factor of n, is an integer which evenly divides n without leaving a remainder.
a. Thing
b. Divisor0
c. Undefined
d. Undefined

81. In mathematics, the _____ of two non-zero integers, is the largest positive integer that divides both numbers without remainder.
a. Thing
b. Greatest common divisor0
c. Undefined
d. Undefined

82. In mathematics, the conjugate _____ or adjoint matrix of an m-by-n matrix A with complex entries is the n-by-m matrix A* obtained from A by taking the transpose and then taking the complex conjugate of each entry.
a. Thing
b. Pairs0
c. Undefined
d. Undefined

83. In finance, a _____ is collateral that the holder of a position in securities, options, or futures contracts has to deposit to cover the credit risk of his counterparty.
a. Margin0
b. Thing
c. Undefined
d. Undefined

84. The term _____ can refer to an integer which is the square of some other integer, or an algebraic expression that can be factored as the square of some other expression.
a. Thing
b. Perfect square0
c. Undefined
d. Undefined

85. A _____ is a negotiable instrument instructing a financial institution to pay a specific amount of a specific currency from a specific demand account held in the maker/depositor's name with that institution. Both the maker and payee may be natural persons or legal entities.
a. Thing
b. Check0
c. Undefined
d. Undefined

86. _____ are of a number n in its third power-the result of multiplying it by itself three times.
a. Cubes0
b. Thing
c. Undefined
d. Undefined

Chapter 5. Exponents and Polynomials

87. A _____ is a number which is the cube of an integer.
    a. Thing
    b. Perfect cube0
    c. Undefined
    d. Undefined

88. _____ interest refers to the fact that whenever interest is calculated, it is based not only on the original principal, but also on any unpaid interest that has been added to the principal.
    a. Thing
    b. Compound0
    c. Undefined
    d. Undefined

89. _____ refers to the fact that whenever interest is calculated, it is based not only on the original principal, but also on any unpaid interest that has been added to the principal. The more frequently interest is compounded, the faster the balance grows.
    a. Concept
    b. Compound interest0
    c. Undefined
    d. Undefined

90. In mathematics, a _____ is a polynomial equation of the second degree. The general form is $ax^2 + bx + c = 0$.
    a. Thing
    b. Quadratic equation0
    c. Undefined
    d. Undefined

91. Two mathematical objects are equal if and only if they are precisely the same in every way. This defines a binary relation, _____, denoted by the sign of _____ "=" in such a way that the statement "x = y" means that x and y are equal.
    a. Equality0
    b. Thing
    c. Undefined
    d. Undefined

92. The word _____ comes from the Latin word linearis, which means created by lines.
    a. Thing
    b. Linear0
    c. Undefined
    d. Undefined

93. A _____ is an equation in which each term is either a constant or the product of a constant times the first power of a variable.
    a. Linear equation0
    b. Thing
    c. Undefined
    d. Undefined

94. _____ means in succession or back-to-back
    a. Thing
    b. Consecutive0
    c. Undefined
    d. Undefined

95. _____ forms part of thinking. Considered the most complex of all intellectual functions, _____ has been defined as higher-order cognitive process that requires the modulation and control of more routine or fundamental skills.
    a. Thing
    b. Problem solving0
    c. Undefined
    d. Undefined

96. A _____ is one of the basic shapes of geometry: a polygon with three vertices and three sides which are straight line segments.

a. Triangle0
b. Thing
c. Undefined
d. Undefined

97. _____ has one 90° internal angle a right angle.
a. Thing
b. Right triangle0
c. Undefined
d. Undefined

98. _____ is a relation in Euclidean geometry among the three sides of a right triangle.
a. Pythagorean Theorem0
b. Thing
c. Undefined
d. Undefined

99. In mathematics, a _____ is a statement that can be proved on the basis of explicitly stated or previously agreed assumptions.
a. Thing
b. Theorem0
c. Undefined
d. Undefined

100. In a right triangle, the _____ of the triangle are the two sides that are perpendicular to each other, as opposed to the hypotenuse.
a. Thing
b. Legs0
c. Undefined
d. Undefined

101. The _____ of a right triangle is the triangle's longest side; the side opposite the right angle.
a. Hypotenuse0
b. Thing
c. Undefined
d. Undefined

102. Initial objects are also called _____, and terminal objects are also called final.
a. Coterminal0
b. Thing
c. Undefined
d. Undefined

103. In geometry, a _____ is defined as a quadrilateral where all four of its angles are right angles.
a. Rectangle0
b. Thing
c. Undefined
d. Undefined

104. A _____ is any object propelled through space by the applicationp of a force.
a. Projectile0
b. Thing
c. Undefined
d. Undefined

105. _____ is the path a moving object follows through space.
a. Projectile motion0
b. Thing
c. Undefined
d. Undefined

106. A _____ is a set of possible values that a variable can take on in order to satisfy a given set of conditions, which may include equations and inequalities.
a. Thing
b. Solution set0
c. Undefined
d. Undefined

Chapter 5. Exponents and Polynomials

107. The _____ integers are all the integers from zero on upwards.
   a. Thing
   b. Nonnegative0
   c. Undefined
   d. Undefined

108. In mathematics, an _____ is a statement about the relative size or order of two objects.
   a. Inequality0
   b. Thing
   c. Undefined
   d. Undefined

109. In mathematics, the multiplicative inverse of a number x, denoted 1/x or x^{-1}, is the number which, when multiplied by x, yields 1. The multiplicative inverse of x is also called the _____ of x.
   a. Reciprocal0
   b. Thing
   c. Undefined
   d. Undefined

110. _____ is often used to describe the measurement of the steepness, incline, gradient, or grade of a straight line. The _____ is defined as the ratio of the "rise" divided by the "run" between two points on a line, or in other words, the ratio of the altitude change to the horizontal distance between any two points on the line.
   a. Slope0
   b. Thing
   c. Undefined
   d. Undefined

111. In elementary algebra, an _____ is a set that contains every real number between two indicated numbers and may contain the two numbers themselves.
   a. Thing
   b. Interval0
   c. Undefined
   d. Undefined

112. _____ is the notation in which permitted values for a variable are expressed as ranging over a certain interval; "5 < x < 9" is an example of the application of _____.
   a. Interval notation0
   b. Thing
   c. Undefined
   d. Undefined

113. In mathematics, a _____ is an ordered list of objects. Like a set, it contains members, also called elements or terms, and the number of terms is called the length of the _____. Unlike a set, order matters, and the exact same elements can appear multiple times at different positions in the _____.
   a. Thing
   b. Sequence0
   c. Undefined
   d. Undefined

114. An _____ or member of a set is an object that when collected together make up the set.
   a. Thing
   b. Element0
   c. Undefined
   d. Undefined

115. In mathematics, the _____, or members of a set or more generally a class are all those objects which when collected together make up the set or class.
   a. Elements0
   b. Thing
   c. Undefined
   d. Undefined

116. In mathematics, a _____ number is a number which can be expressed as a ratio of two integers. Non-integer _____ numbers (commonly called fractions) are usually written as the vulgar fraction a / b, where b is not zero.

a. Rational0
b. Thing
c. Undefined
d. Undefined

117. In geometry, the _____ of an object is a point in some sense in the middle of the object.
    a. Center0
    b. Thing
    c. Undefined
    d. Undefined

118. In Euclidean geometry, a _____ is the set of all points in a plane at a fixed distance, called the radius, from a given point, the center.
    a. Thing
    b. Circle0
    c. Undefined
    d. Undefined

119. Blaise _____ was a French mathematician, physicist, and religious philosopher.
    a. Person
    b. Pascal0
    c. Undefined
    d. Undefined

120. Leonardo of Pisa (1170s or 1180s – 1250), also known as Leonardo Pisano, Leonardo Bonacci, Leonardo _____, or, most commonly, simply _____, was an Italian mathematician, considered by some "the most talented mathematician of the Middle Ages."
    a. Person
    b. Fibonacci0
    c. Undefined
    d. Undefined

121. In computer science an _____ is a data structure that consists of a group of elements having a single name that are accessed by indexing. In most programming languages each element has the same data type and the _____ occupies a continuous area of storage.
    a. Array0
    b. Thing
    c. Undefined
    d. Undefined

122. A _____ can refer to a line joining two nonadjacent vertices of a polygon or polyhedron, or in some contexts any upward or downward sloping line. .
    a. Thing
    b. Diagonal0
    c. Undefined
    d. Undefined

123. In mathematics, a _____ is any function which can be written as the ratio of two polynomial functions.
    a. Thing
    b. Rational function0
    c. Undefined
    d. Undefined

124. A _____ is an abstract model that uses mathematical language to describe the behavior of a system. Eykhoff defined a _____ as 'a representation of the essential aspects of an existing system which presents knowledge of that system in usable form'.
    a. Mathematical model0
    b. Thing
    c. Undefined
    d. Undefined

Chapter 6. Rational Expressions and Rational functions

1. In set theory and its applications throughout mathematics, _____ are a collection of sets (or sometimes other mathematical objects) that can be unambiguously defined by a property that all its members share.
   a. Classes0
   b. Thing
   c. Undefined
   d. Undefined

2. In mathematics, there are several meanings of _____ depending on the subject.
   a. Thing
   b. Degree0
   c. Undefined
   d. Undefined

3. A _____ is a numeral used to indicate a count. The most common use of the word today is to name the part of a fraction that tells the number or count of equal parts.
   a. Thing
   b. Numerator0
   c. Undefined
   d. Undefined

4. In mathematics, a _____ number is a number which can be expressed as a ratio of two integers. Non-integer _____ numbers (commonly called fractions) are usually written as the vulgar fraction a / b, where b is not zero.
   a. Thing
   b. Rational0
   c. Undefined
   d. Undefined

5. Equivalence is the condition of being _____ or essentially equal.
   a. Thing
   b. Equivalent0
   c. Undefined
   d. Undefined

6. An _____ is a combination of numbers, operators, grouping symbols and/or free variables and bound variables arranged in a meaningful way which can be evaluated..
   a. Thing
   b. Expression0
   c. Undefined
   d. Undefined

7. A _____ is the part of a fraction that tells how many equal parts make up a whole, and which is used in the name of the fraction: "halves", "thirds", "fourths" or "quarters", "fifths" and so on.
   a. Concept
   b. Denominator0
   c. Undefined
   d. Undefined

8. In mathematics, a _____ is an expression that is constructed from one or more variables and constants, using only the operations of addition, subtraction, multiplication, and constant positive whole number exponents. is a _____. Note in particular that division by an expression containing a variable is not in general allowed in polynomials. [1]
   a. Polynomial0
   b. Thing
   c. Undefined
   d. Undefined

9. In mathematics, _____ is the decomposition of an object into a product of other objects, or factors, which when multiplied together give the original.
   a. Factoring0
   b. Thing
   c. Undefined
   d. Undefined

10. A _____ is a symbolic representation denoting a quantity or expression. It often represents an "unknown" quantity that has the potential to change.

Chapter 6. Rational Expressions and Rational functions

a. Thing
b. Variable0
c. Undefined
d. Undefined

11. In mathematics, a _____ may be described informally as a number that can be given by an infinite decimal representation.
a. Thing
b. Real number0
c. Undefined
d. Undefined

12. In financial mathematics, the _____ volatility of an option contract is the volatility _____ by the market price of the option based on an option pricing model.
a. Thing
b. Implied0
c. Undefined
d. Undefined

13. In mathematics, factorization (British English: factorisation) or factoring is the decomposition of an object (for example, a number, a polynomial, or a matrix) into a product of other objects, or _____, which when multiplied together give the original.
a. Thing
b. Factors0
c. Undefined
d. Undefined

14. _____ is the largest positive integer that divides both numbers without remainder.
a. Thing
b. Common Factor0
c. Undefined
d. Undefined

15. In Euclidean geometry, a _____ is the set of all points in a plane at a fixed distance, called the radius, from a given point, the center.
a. Circle0
b. Thing
c. Undefined
d. Undefined

16. A _____ is a quantity that denotes the proportional amount or magnitude of one quantity relative to another.
a. Ratio0
b. Thing
c. Undefined
d. Undefined

17. The _____ is the distance around a closed curve. _____ is a kind of perimeter.
a. Circumference0
b. Thing
c. Undefined
d. Undefined

18. In geometry, a _____ (Greek words diairo = divide and metro = measure) of a circle is any straight line segment that passes through the centre and whose endpoints are on the circular boundary, or, in more modern usage, the length of such a line segment. When using the word in the more modern sense, one speaks of the _____ rather than a _____, because all diameters of a circle have the same length. This length is twice the radius. The _____ of a circle is also the longest chord that the circle has.
a. Thing
b. Diameter0
c. Undefined
d. Undefined

19. In mathematics, an _____, mean, or central tendency of a data set refers to a measure of the "middle" or "expected" value of the data set.

Chapter 6. Rational Expressions and Rational functions

    a. Concept
    c. Undefined
    b. Average0
    d. Undefined

20. _____ is the transport of people on a trip/journey or the process or time involved in a person or object moving from one location to another.
    a. Travel0
    b. Thing
    c. Undefined
    d. Undefined

21. A _____ is a special kind of ratio, indicating a relationship between two measurements with different units, such as miles to gallons or cents to pounds.
    a. Rate0
    b. Thing
    c. Undefined
    d. Undefined

22. A _____ is a unit of length, usually used to measure distance, in a number of different systems, including Imperial units, United States customary units and Norwegian/Swedish mil. Its size can vary from system to system, but in each is between 1 and 10 kilometers. In contemporary English contexts _____ refers to either:
    a. Thing
    b. Mile0
    c. Undefined
    d. Undefined

23. _____ is a unit of speed, expressing the number of international miles covered per hour.
    a. Thing
    b. Miles per hour0
    c. Undefined
    d. Undefined

24. _____ is a kind of property which exists as magnitude or multitude. It is among the basic classes of things along with quality, substance, change, and relation.
    a. Thing
    b. Amount0
    c. Undefined
    d. Undefined

25. _____ are a measure of time.
    a. Minutes0
    b. Thing
    c. Undefined
    d. Undefined

26. The mathematical concept of a _____ expresses the intuitive idea of deterministic dependence between two quantities, one of which is viewed as primary and the other as secondary. A _____ then is a way to associate a unique output for each input of a specified type, for example, a real number or an element of a given set.
    a. Function0
    b. Thing
    c. Undefined
    d. Undefined

27. In mathematics, a _____ is any function which can be written as the ratio of two polynomial functions.
    a. Rational function0
    b. Thing
    c. Undefined
    d. Undefined

28. In mathematics, a _____ of a k-place relation $L \subseteq X_1 \times ... \times X_k$ is one of the sets X_j, $1 \leq j \leq k$. In the special case where k = 2 and $L \subseteq X_1 \times X_2$ is a function $L : X_1 \rightarrow X_2$, it is conventional to refer to X_1 as the _____ of the function and to refer to X_2 as the codomain of the function.

Chapter 6. Rational Expressions and Rational functions

a. Domain0
b. Thing
c. Undefined
d. Undefined

29. _____ are the basic objects of study in graph theory. Informally speaking, a graph is a set of objects called points, nodes, or vertices connected by links called lines or edges.
    a. Thing
    b. Graphs0
    c. Undefined
    d. Undefined

30. _____, or Fuel efficiency can sometimes mean the same as thermal efficiency, that is, the efficiency of converting energy contained in a carrier fuel to kinetic energy or work.
    a. Fuel consumption0
    b. Thing
    c. Undefined
    d. Undefined

31. U.S. liquid _____ is legally defined as 231 cubic inches, and is equal to 3.785411784 litres or abotu 0.13368 cubic feet. This is the most common definition of a _____. The U.S. fluid ounce is defined as 1/128 of a U.S. _____.
    a. Thing
    b. Gallon0
    c. Undefined
    d. Undefined

32. In plane geometry, a _____ is a polygon with four equal sides, four right angles, and parallel opposite sides. In algebra, the _____ of a number is that number multiplied by itself.
    a. Thing
    b. Square0
    c. Undefined
    d. Undefined

33. _____ is electromagnetic radiation with a wavelength that is visible to the eye (visible _____) or, in a technical or scientific context, electromagnetic radiation of any wavelength.
    a. Light0
    b. Thing
    c. Undefined
    d. Undefined

34. In geometry, the _____ of an object is a point in some sense in the middle of the object.
    a. Center0
    b. Thing
    c. Undefined
    d. Undefined

35. A _____ is a negotiable instrument instructing a financial institution to pay a specific amount of a specific currency from a specific demand account held in the maker/depositor's name with that institution. Both the maker and payee may be natural persons or legal entities.
    a. Check0
    b. Thing
    c. Undefined
    d. Undefined

36. In mathematics, a _____ function in the sense of algebraic geometry is an everywhere-defined, polynomial function on an algebraic variety V with values in the field K over which V is defined.
    a. Regular0
    b. Thing
    c. Undefined
    d. Undefined

37. In mathematics, a _____ is a particular kind of polynomial, having just one term.

Chapter 6. Rational Expressions and Rational functions

    a. Monomial0
    c. Undefined
    b. Thing
    d. Undefined

38. In mathematics, and in particular in abstract algebra, the _____ is a property of binary operations that generalises the distributive law from elementary algebra.
    a. Distributive property0
    c. Undefined
    b. Thing
    d. Undefined

39. In mathematics, a _____ is a constant multiplicative factor of a certain object. The object can be such things as a variable, a vector, a function, etc. For example, the _____ of $9x^2$ is 9.
    a. Coefficient0
    c. Undefined
    b. Thing
    d. Undefined

40. _____ is a mathematical operation, written a^n, involving two numbers, the base a and the exponent n.
    a. Exponentiating0
    c. Undefined
    b. Thing
    d. Undefined

41. _____ is a mathematical operation, written a^n, involving two numbers, the base a and the exponent n.
    a. Thing
    c. Undefined
    b. Exponentiation0
    d. Undefined

42. In mathematics, a _____ is the result of multiplying, or an expression that identifies factors to be multiplied.
    a. Thing
    c. Undefined
    b. Product0
    d. Undefined

43. In mathematics, a _____ is the end result of a division problem. It can also be expressed as the number of times the divisor divides into the dividend.
    a. Quotient0
    c. Undefined
    b. Thing
    d. Undefined

44. The function difference divided by the point difference is known as the _____
    a. Difference quotient0
    c. Undefined
    b. Thing
    d. Undefined

45. In mathematics, a _____ can mean either an element of the set {1, 2, 3, ...} (i.e the positive integers) or an element of the set {0, 1, 2, 3, ...} (i.e. the non-negative integers).
    a. Whole number0
    c. Undefined
    b. Concept
    d. Undefined

46. In arithmetic, _____ is a procedure for calculating the division of one integer, called the dividend, by another integer called the divisor, to produce a result called the quotient.
    a. Long division0
    c. Undefined
    b. Thing
    d. Undefined

Chapter 6. Rational Expressions and Rational functions

47. In mathematics, the additive inverse, or _____ of a number n is the number that, when added to n, yields zero. The additive inverse of n is denoted −n. For example, 7 is −7, because 7 + (−7) = 0, and the additive inverse of −0.3 is 0.3, because −0.3 + 0.3 = 0.
   a. Thing
   b. Opposite0
   c. Undefined
   d. Undefined

48. In mathematics, the _____ of a number n is the number that, when added to n, yields zero. The _____ of n is denoted −n. For example, 7 is −7, because 7 + (−7) = 0, and the _____ of −0.3 is 0.3, because −0.3 + 0.3 = 0.
   a. Additive inverse0
   b. Thing
   c. Undefined
   d. Undefined

49. A _____ is the part of the dividend that is left over when the dividend is not evenly divisible by the divisor.
   a. Remainder0
   b. Thing
   c. Undefined
   d. Undefined

50. _____ has many meanings, most of which simply .
   a. Thing
   b. Power0
   c. Undefined
   d. Undefined

51. In mathematics and the mathematical sciences, a _____ is a fixed, but possibly unspecified, value. This is in contrast to a variable, which is not fixed.
   a. Constant0
   b. Thing
   c. Undefined
   d. Undefined

52. _____ is a fixed, but possibly unspecified, value. This is in contrast to a variable, which is not fixed.
   a. Thing
   b. Constant term0
   c. Undefined
   d. Undefined

53. A _____ is a polynomial consisting of three terms; in other words, it is the sum of three monomials.
   a. Thing
   b. Trinomial0
   c. Undefined
   d. Undefined

54. _____ in algebra is an application of polynomial long division.
   a. Thing
   b. Remainder theorem0
   c. Undefined
   d. Undefined

55. _____ is a branch of mathematics concerning the study of structure, relation and quantity.
   a. Concept
   b. Algebra0
   c. Undefined
   d. Undefined

56. In mathematics, a _____ is a statement that can be proved on the basis of explicitly stated or previously agreed assumptions.
   a. Theorem0
   b. Thing
   c. Undefined
   d. Undefined

Chapter 6. Rational Expressions and Rational functions

57. Fixed costs are expenses whose total does not change in proportion to the activity of a business.Unit fixed costs decline with volume following a retangular hyperbola as the volume of production.Variable costs by contrast change in relation to the activity of a business such as sales or production volume.Along with variable costs,fixed costs make up one of the two components of total cost. In the most simple production function total cost is equal to fixed costs plus variable costs.In accounting terminology, fixed costs will broadly include all costs which are not included in cost of goods sold, and variable costs are those captured in costs of goods sold. The implicit assumption required to make the equivalence between the accounting and economics terminology is that the accounting period is equal to the period in which fixed costs do not vary in relation to production. In practice, this equivalence does not always hold and depending on the period under consideration by management, some overhead expenses can be adjusted by management, and the specific allocation of each expense to each category will be decided under cost accounting.In business planning and management accounting, usage of the terms fixed costs, variable costs and others will often differ from usage in economics, and may depend on the intended use. For example, costs may be segregated into per unit costs fixed costs per period, and variable costs as a proportion of revenue. Capital expenditures will usually be allocated separately, and depending on the purpose, a portion may be regularly allocated to expenses as depreciation and amortization and seen as a _____ per period, or the entire amount may be considered upfront fixed costs.
   a. Thing
   b. Fixed cost0
   c. Undefined
   d. Undefined

58. _____ are expenses whose total does not change in proportion to the activity of a business, within the relevant time period or scale of production
   a. Fixed costs0
   b. Thing
   c. Undefined
   d. Undefined

59. In mathematics, _____ is an elementary arithmetic operation. When one of the numbers is a whole number, _____ is the repeated sum of the other number.
   a. Thing
   b. Multiplication0
   c. Undefined
   d. Undefined

60. In mathematics, the multiplicative inverse of a number x, denoted 1/x or x^{-1}, is the number which, when multiplied by x, yields 1. The multiplicative inverse of x is also called the _____ of x.
   a. Thing
   b. Reciprocal0
   c. Undefined
   d. Undefined

61. In abstract algebra, _____ consists of sets with binary operations that satisfy certain axioms.
   a. Grouping0
   b. Thing
   c. Undefined
   d. Undefined

62. _____ is a business term for the amount of money that a company receives from its activities in a given period, mostly from sales of products and/or services to customers
   a. Revenue0
   b. Thing
   c. Undefined
   d. Undefined

63. In economics, supply and _____ describe market relations between prospective sellers and buyers of a good.
   a. Thing
   b. Demand0
   c. Undefined
   d. Undefined

Chapter 6. Rational Expressions and Rational functions

64. In mathematics, a _____ is a quadric surface, with the following equation in Cartesian coordinates: $(x/a)^2 + (y/b)^2 = 1$.
   a. Thing
   b. Cylinder0
   c. Undefined
   d. Undefined

65. A _____ surface is the surface or face of a solid on its sides. It can also be defined as any face or surface that is not a base.
   a. Lateral0
   b. Thing
   c. Undefined
   d. Undefined

66. A _____ is the result of the addition of a set of numbers. The numbers may be natural numbers, complex numbers, matrices, or still more complicated objects. An infinite _____ is a subtle procedure known as a series.
   a. Thing
   b. Sum0
   c. Undefined
   d. Undefined

67. _____, either of the curved-bracket punctuation marks that together make a set of _____
   a. Thing
   b. Parentheses0
   c. Undefined
   d. Undefined

68. In mathematics, a _____ of an integer n, also called a factor of n, is an integer which evenly divides n without leaving a remainder.
   a. Thing
   b. Divisor0
   c. Undefined
   d. Undefined

69. In mathematics, a _____ number (or a _____) is a natural number that has exactly two (distinct) natural number divisors, which are 1 and the _____ number itself.
   a. Prime0
   b. Thing
   c. Undefined
   d. Undefined

70. The _____ of a positive integer are the prime numbers that divide into that integer exactly, without leaving a remainder. The process of finding these numbers is called integer factorization, or prime factorization.
   a. Thing
   b. Prime factor0
   c. Undefined
   d. Undefined

71. The _____ are the only integral domain whose positive elements are well-ordered, and in which order is preserved by addition. Like the natural numbers, the _____ form a countably infinite set. The set of all _____ is usually denoted in mathematics by a boldface Z .
   a. Integers0
   b. Thing
   c. Undefined
   d. Undefined

72. _____ means in succession or back-to-back
   a. Thing
   b. Consecutive0
   c. Undefined
   d. Undefined

73. In physics, an _____ is the path that an object makes around another object while under the influence of a source of centripetal force, such as gravity.

Chapter 6. Rational Expressions and Rational functions 79

    a. Thing
    b. Orbit0
    c. Undefined
    d. Undefined

74. _____ of an object is its speed in a particular direction.
    a. Thing
    b. Velocity0
    c. Undefined
    d. Undefined

75. Mathematical _____ is used to represent ideas.
    a. Notation0
    b. Thing
    c. Undefined
    d. Undefined

76. _____ is a notation for writing numbers that is often used by scientists and mathematicians to make it easier to write large and small numbers.
    a. Scientific notation0
    b. Thing
    c. Undefined
    d. Undefined

77. The _____ of an algebraic expression is the same equation, but without parentheses.
    a. Expanded form0
    b. Thing
    c. Undefined
    d. Undefined

78. In mathematics, _____ expressions is used to reduce the expression into the lowest possible term.
    a. Thing
    b. Simplifying0
    c. Undefined
    d. Undefined

79. In statistics the _____ of an event i is the number n_i of times the event occurred in the experiment or the study. These frequencies are often graphically represented in histograms.
    a. Frequency0
    b. Concept
    c. Undefined
    d. Undefined

80. The _____ is the change in frequency and wavelength of a wave that is perceived by an observer moving relative to the source of the waves
    a. Doppler Effect0
    b. Thing
    c. Undefined
    d. Undefined

81. In mathematics and more specifically set theory, the _____ set is the unique set which contains no elements.
    a. Thing
    b. Empty0
    c. Undefined
    d. Undefined

82. A _____ is a set of possible values that a variable can take on in order to satisfy a given set of conditions, which may include equations and inequalities.
    a. Thing
    b. Solution set0
    c. Undefined
    d. Undefined

83. Two mathematical objects are equal if and only if they are precisely the same in every way. This defines a binary relation, _____, denoted by the sign of _____ "=" in such a way that the statement "x = y" means that x and y are equal.

a. Thing
b. Equality0
c. Undefined
d. Undefined

84. The _____, the average in everyday English, which is also called the arithmetic _____ (and is distinguished from the geometric _____ or harmonic _____). The average is also called the sample _____. The expected value of a random variable, which is also called the population _____.
a. Thing
b. Mean0
c. Undefined
d. Undefined

85. _____ variables are variables other than the independent variable that may bear any effect on the behavior of the subject being studied.
a. Extraneous0
b. Thing
c. Undefined
d. Undefined

86. In common philosophical language, a proposition or _____, is the content of an assertion, that is, it is true-or-false and defined by the meaning of a particular piece of language.
a. Statement0
b. Concept
c. Undefined
d. Undefined

87. An _____ is an equality that remains true regardless of the values of any variables that appear within it, to distinguish it from an equality which is true under more particular conditions.
a. Thing
b. Identity0
c. Undefined
d. Undefined

88. In acoustics and telecommunication, the _____ of a wave is a component frequency of the signal that is an integer multiple of the fundamental frequency.
a. Thing
b. Harmonic0
c. Undefined
d. Undefined

89. The _____ is one of several kinds of average. It is the number of variables divided by the sum of the reciprocals of the variables.
a. Harmonic mean0
b. Thing
c. Undefined
d. Undefined

90. A _____ is one of the basic shapes of geometry: a polygon with three vertices and three sides which are straight line segments.
a. Triangle0
b. Thing
c. Undefined
d. Undefined

91. A _____ signifies a point or points of probability on a subject e.g., the _____ of creativity, which allows for the formation of rule or norm or law by interpretation of the phenomena events that can be created.
a. Principle0
b. Thing
c. Undefined
d. Undefined

92. In mathematics, a _____ is a two-dimensional manifold or surface that is perfectly flat.

a. Thing
b. Plane0
c. Undefined
d. Undefined

93. In geometry, a _____ is defined as a quadrilateral where all four of its angles are right angles.
    a. Rectangle0
    b. Thing
    c. Undefined
    d. Undefined

94. _____ has one 90° internal angle a right angle.
    a. Right triangle0
    b. Thing
    c. Undefined
    d. Undefined

95. In mathematics, _____ are essentially word problems that are designed to use mathematical critical thinking in everyday situations.
    a. Application problems0
    b. Thing
    c. Undefined
    d. Undefined

96. The _____ of measurement are a globally standardized and modernized form of the metric system.
    a. Units0
    b. Thing
    c. Undefined
    d. Undefined

97. _____ is a concept in traditional logic referring to a "type of immediate inference in which from a given proposition another proposition is inferred which has as its subject the predicate of the original proposition and as its predicate the subject of the original proposition (the quality of the proposition being retained)."
    a. Concept
    b. Conversion0
    c. Undefined
    d. Undefined

98. A _____ is a function that assigns a number to subsets of a given set.
    a. Measure0
    b. Thing
    c. Undefined
    d. Undefined

99. _____ forms part of thinking. Considered the most complex of all intellectual functions, _____ has been defined as higher-order cognitive process that requires the modulation and control of more routine or fundamental skills.
    a. Thing
    b. Problem solving0
    c. Undefined
    d. Undefined

100. In botany, _____ are above-ground plant organs specialized for photosynthesis. Their characteristics are typically analyzed by using Fiobonacci's sequences.
    a. Leaves0
    b. Thing
    c. Undefined
    d. Undefined

101. In mathematics, _____ are two-dimensional manifolds or surfaces that are perfectly flat.
    a. Planes0
    b. Thing
    c. Undefined
    d. Undefined

102. The _____ of a solid object is the three-dimensional concept of how much space it occupies, often quantified numerically.

Chapter 6. Rational Expressions and Rational functions

a. Thing
b. Volume0
c. Undefined
d. Undefined

103. The metre (or _____, see spelling differences) is a measure of length. It is the basic unit of length in the metric system and in the International System of Units (SI), used around the world for general and scientific purposes.
a. Meter0
b. Concept
c. Undefined
d. Undefined

104. The system of _____ numerals was a numeral system used in ancient Egypt. It was a decimal system, often rounded off to the higher power, written in hieroglyphs.
a. Thing
b. Egyptian0
c. Undefined
d. Undefined

105. The _____ , is named after Alexander Henry Rhind, a Scottish antiquarian, who purchased the papyrus in 1858 in Luxor, Egypt; it was apparently found during illegal excavations in or near the Ramesseum.
a. Thing
b. Rhind papyrus0
c. Undefined
d. Undefined

106. _____ mathematical functions take numeric arguments and produce numeric results.
a. Thing
b. Miscellaneous0
c. Undefined
d. Undefined

107. In mathematics, a _____ is a number which can be expressed as a ratio of two integers. Non-integer rational numbers (commonly called fractions) are usually written as the vulgar fraction a / b, where b is not zero.
a. Concept
b. Rational Number0
c. Undefined
d. Undefined

108. _____ are objects, characters, or other concrete representations of ideas, concepts, or other abstractions.
a. Thing
b. Symbols0
c. Undefined
d. Undefined

109. In mathematics, an _____ is a statement about the relative size or order of two objects.
a. Thing
b. Inequality0
c. Undefined
d. Undefined

110. A _____ is a set of numbers that designate location in a given reference system, such as x,y in a planar _____ system or an x,y,z in a three-dimensional _____ system.
a. Thing
b. Coordinate0
c. Undefined
d. Undefined

111. In mathematics and its applications, a _____ is a system for assigning an n-tuple of numbers or scalars to each point in an n-dimensional space.
a. Concept
b. Coordinate system0
c. Undefined
d. Undefined

Chapter 6. Rational Expressions and Rational functions 83

112. In mathematics, an inequality is a statement about the relative size or order of two objects. For example 14 > 10, or 14 is _____ 10.
 a. Thing
 b. Greater than0
 c. Undefined
 d. Undefined

113. In mathematics, a _____ is an ordered list of objects. Like a set, it contains members, also called elements or terms, and the number of terms is called the length of the _____. Unlike a set, order matters, and the exact same elements can appear multiple times at different positions in the _____.
 a. Sequence0
 b. Thing
 c. Undefined
 d. Undefined

114. _____ or arithmetics is the oldest and most elementary branch of mathematics, used by almost everyone, for tasks ranging from simple daily counting to advanced science and business calculations.
 a. Thing
 b. Arithmetic0
 c. Undefined
 d. Undefined

115. Acid _____ ratio measures the ability of a company to use its near cash or quick assets to immediately extinguish its current liabilities.
 a. Test0
 b. Thing
 c. Undefined
 d. Undefined

116. _____ is a mathematical science pertaining to the collection, analysis, interpretation or explanation, and presentation of data. It is applicable to a wide variety of academic disciplines, from the physical and social sciences to the humanities.
 a. Thing
 b. Statistics0
 c. Undefined
 d. Undefined

Chapter 7. Rational Exponents and Roots

1. _____ is the fee paid on borrowed money.
   a. Thing
   b. Interest0
   c. Undefined
   d. Undefined

2. The metre (or _____, see spelling differences) is a measure of length. It is the basic unit of length in the metric system and in the International System of Units (SI), used around the world for general and scientific purposes.
   a. Concept
   b. Meter0
   c. Undefined
   d. Undefined

3. _____ is a relation in Euclidean geometry among the three sides of a right triangle.
   a. Thing
   b. Pythagorean Theorem0
   c. Undefined
   d. Undefined

4. In geometry, a _____ is defined as a quadrilateral where all four of its angles are right angles.
   a. Rectangle0
   b. Thing
   c. Undefined
   d. Undefined

5. In plane geometry, a _____ is a polygon with four equal sides, four right angles, and parallel opposite sides. In algebra, the _____ of a number is that number multiplied by itself.
   a. Square0
   b. Thing
   c. Undefined
   d. Undefined

6. In mathematics, a _____ of a number x is a number r such that $r^2 = x$, or in words, a number r whose square (the result of multiplying the number by itself) is x.
   a. Thing
   b. Square root0
   c. Undefined
   d. Undefined

7. In mathematics, a _____ of a complex-valued function f is a member x of the domain of f such that f(x) vanishes at x, that is, x : f (x) = 0.
   a. Root0
   b. Thing
   c. Undefined
   d. Undefined

8. In mathematics, a _____ is a statement that can be proved on the basis of explicitly stated or previously agreed assumptions.
   a. Thing
   b. Theorem0
   c. Undefined
   d. Undefined

9. A _____ can refer to a line joining two nonadjacent vertices of a polygon or polyhedron, or in some contexts any upward or downward sloping line. .
   a. Thing
   b. Diagonal0
   c. Undefined
   d. Undefined

10. A _____ is a three-dimensional solid object bounded by six square faces, facets, or sides, with three meeting at each vertex.
    a. Cube0
    b. Thing
    c. Undefined
    d. Undefined

Chapter 7. Rational Exponents and Roots

11. A _____ is a rectangle whose side lengths are in the golden ratio, 1:, that is, approximately 1:1.618.
    a. Golden rectangle0
    b. Thing
    c. Undefined
    d. Undefined

12. Mathematical _____ is used to represent ideas.
    a. Thing
    b. Notation0
    c. Undefined
    d. Undefined

13. _____ is a mathematical operation, written a^n, involving two numbers, the base a and the exponent n.
    a. Exponentiating0
    b. Thing
    c. Undefined
    d. Undefined

14. _____ is a mathematical operation, written a^n, involving two numbers, the base a and the exponent n.
    a. Thing
    b. Exponentiation0
    c. Undefined
    d. Undefined

15. _____ has many meanings, most of which simply .
    a. Power0
    b. Thing
    c. Undefined
    d. Undefined

16. The _____ integers are all the integers from zero on upwards.
    a. Nonnegative0
    b. Thing
    c. Undefined
    d. Undefined

17. _____ is the symbol used to indicate the nth root of a number
    a. Radical0
    b. Thing
    c. Undefined
    d. Undefined

18. An _____ is a combination of numbers, operators, grouping symbols and/or free variables and bound variables arranged in a meaningful way which can be evaluated..
    a. Thing
    b. Expression0
    c. Undefined
    d. Undefined

19. The _____ is the number or expression underneath the radical sign.
    a. Thing
    b. Radicand0
    c. Undefined
    d. Undefined

20. The word _____ is used in a variety of ways in mathematics.
    a. Index0
    b. Thing
    c. Undefined
    d. Undefined

21. A _____ is a number that is less than zero.
    a. Negative number0
    b. Thing
    c. Undefined
    d. Undefined

Chapter 7. Rational Exponents and Roots

22. In mathematics, an inequality is a statement about the relative size or order of two objects. For example 14 > 10, or 14 is _____ 10.
    a. Thing
    b. Greater than0
    c. Undefined
    d. Undefined

23. In mathematics, _____ are used to indicate the square root of a number.
    a. Radicals0
    b. Thing
    c. Undefined
    d. Undefined

24. In mathematics, a _____ may be described informally as a number that can be given by an infinite decimal representation.
    a. Real number0
    b. Thing
    c. Undefined
    d. Undefined

25. A _____ is a symbolic representation denoting a quantity or expression. It often represents an "unknown" quantity that has the potential to change.
    a. Thing
    b. Variable0
    c. Undefined
    d. Undefined

26. A _____ of a number is a number a such that $a^3 = x$.
    a. Thing
    b. Cube root0
    c. Undefined
    d. Undefined

27. In mathematics, a _____ number is a number which can be expressed as a ratio of two integers. Non-integer _____ numbers (commonly called fractions) are usually written as the vulgar fraction a / b, where b is not zero.
    a. Thing
    b. Rational0
    c. Undefined
    d. Undefined

28. An _____ of a number a is a number b such that $b^n = a$.
    a. Thing
    b. Nth root0
    c. Undefined
    d. Undefined

29. In mathematics, a _____ is a demonstration that, assuming certain axioms, some statement is necessarily true.
    a. Thing
    b. Proof0
    c. Undefined
    d. Undefined

30. A _____ is one of the basic shapes of geometry: a polygon with three vertices and three sides which are straight line segments.
    a. Triangle0
    b. Thing
    c. Undefined
    d. Undefined

31. A _____ is the result of the addition of a set of numbers. The numbers may be natural numbers, complex numbers, matrices, or still more complicated objects. An infinite _____ is a subtle procedure known as a series.
    a. Sum0
    b. Thing
    c. Undefined
    d. Undefined

32. _____ has one 90° internal angle a right angle.
   a. Thing
   b. Right triangle0
   c. Undefined
   d. Undefined

33. In mathematics, the _____ of a coordinate system is the point where the axes of the system intersect.
   a. Thing
   b. Origin0
   c. Undefined
   d. Undefined

34. In geometry, a line _____ is a part of a line that is bounded by two end points, and contains every point on the line between its end points.
   a. Segment0
   b. Concept
   c. Undefined
   d. Undefined

35. _____, also known as _____ of Alexandria, was a Greek mathematician. His Elements is the most successful textbook in the history of mathematics. In it, the principles of geometry are deduced from a small set of axioms. His method of proving mathematical theorems by logical reasoning from accepted first principles remains the backbone of mathematics and is responsible for the field's characteristic rigor
   a. Euclid0
   b. Person
   c. Undefined
   d. Undefined

36. _____ was a Greek philosopher, a student of Plato and teacher of Alexander the Great. He wrote on diverse subjects, including physics, metaphysics, poetry, biology and zoology, logic, rhetoric, politics, government, and ethics.
   a. Person
   b. Aristotle0
   c. Undefined
   d. Undefined

37. _____ whose original name was Aristocles, was an ancient Greek philosopher, the second of the great trio of ancient Greeks –succeeding Socrates and preceeding Aristotle– who between them laid the philosophical foundations of Western culture.
   a. Person
   b. Plato0
   c. Undefined
   d. Undefined

38. _____ is the middle point of a line segment.
   a. Midpoint0
   b. Thing
   c. Undefined
   d. Undefined

39. An _____ or member of a set is an object that when collected together make up the set.
   a. Element0
   b. Thing
   c. Undefined
   d. Undefined

40. In mathematics, the _____ , or members of a set or more generally a class are all those objects which when collected together make up the set or class.
   a. Thing
   b. Elements0
   c. Undefined
   d. Undefined

41. _____ was an American mathematician, known for his work in geometry and the history of mathematics.

Chapter 7. Rational Exponents and Roots

    a. Howard Eves0   b. Person
    c. Undefined   d. Undefined

42.   A _____ is a quantity that denotes the proportional amount or magnitude of one quantity relative to another.
    a. Ratio0   b. Thing
    c. Undefined   d. Undefined

43.   The _____ is a number often encountered when taking the ratios of distances in simple geometric figures. It is approximately 1.6180339887.
    a. Golden ratio0   b. Thing
    c. Undefined   d. Undefined

44.   _____ are the basic objects of study in graph theory. Informally speaking, a graph is a set of objects called points, nodes, or vertices connected by links called lines or edges.
    a. Thing   b. Graphs0
    c. Undefined   d. Undefined

45.   In mathematics, _____ growth occurs when the growth rate of a function is always proportional to the function's current size.
    a. Exponential0   b. Thing
    c. Undefined   d. Undefined

46.   _____ is the transport of people on a trip/journey or the process or time involved in a person or object moving from one location to another.
    a. Thing   b. Travel0
    c. Undefined   d. Undefined

47.   In classical geometry, a _____ of a circle or sphere is any line segment from its center to its boundary. By extension, the _____ of a circle or sphere is the length of any such segment. The _____ is half the diameter. In science and engineering the term _____ of curvature is commonly used as a synonym for _____.
    a. Radius0   b. Thing
    c. Undefined   d. Undefined

48.   In mathematics, the concept of a _____ tries to capture the intuitive idea of a geometrical one-dimensional and continuous object. A simple example is the circle.
    a. Curve0   b. Thing
    c. Undefined   d. Undefined

49.   A _____ is a unit of length, usually used to measure distance, in a number of different systems, including Imperial units, United States customary units and Norwegian/Swedish mil. Its size can vary from system to system, but in each is between 1 and 10 kilometers. In contemporary English contexts _____ refers to either:
    a. Thing   b. Mile0
    c. Undefined   d. Undefined

50.   _____ is a unit of speed, expressing the number of international miles covered per hour.

Chapter 7. Rational Exponents and Roots

a. Miles per hour0
b. Thing
c. Undefined
d. Undefined

51. In geometry, the _____ of an object is a point in some sense in the middle of the object.
    a. Center0
    b. Thing
    c. Undefined
    d. Undefined

52. In mathematics, _____ expressions is used to reduce the expression into the lowest possible term.
    a. Thing
    b. Simplifying0
    c. Undefined
    d. Undefined

53. In common philosophical language, a proposition or _____, is the content of an assertion, that is, it is true-or-false and defined by the meaning of a particular piece of language.
    a. Statement0
    b. Concept
    c. Undefined
    d. Undefined

54. _____ are objects, characters, or other concrete representations of ideas, concepts, or other abstractions.
    a. Symbols0
    b. Thing
    c. Undefined
    d. Undefined

55. A _____ is a special kind of ratio, indicating a relationship between two measurements with different units, such as miles to gallons or cents to pounds.
    a. Rate0
    b. Thing
    c. Undefined
    d. Undefined

56. An _____ is the fee paid on borrow money.
    a. Interest rate0
    b. Concept
    c. Undefined
    d. Undefined

57. In elementary algebra, a _____ is a polynomial with two terms: the sum of two monomials. It is the simplest kind of polynomial except for a monomial.
    a. Thing
    b. Binomial0
    c. Undefined
    d. Undefined

58. _____ also sometimes known as the double distributive property or more colloquially as foiling, is commonly taught to US high school students learning algebra as a mnemonic for remembering how to multiply two binomials polynomials with two terms.
    a. FOIL method0
    b. Thing
    c. Undefined
    d. Undefined

59. The _____ is commonly taught to US high school students learning algebra as a mnemonic for remembering how to multiply two binomials.
    a. Thing
    b. FOIL rule0
    c. Undefined
    d. Undefined

Chapter 7. Rational Exponents and Roots

60. In mathematics, and in particular in abstract algebra, the _____ is a property of binary operations that generalises the distributive law from elementary algebra.
    a. Distributive property0
    b. Thing
    c. Undefined
    d. Undefined

61. In mathematics, a _____ is the result of multiplying, or an expression that identifies factors to be multiplied.
    a. Thing
    b. Product0
    c. Undefined
    d. Undefined

62. In mathematics the _____ refers to the identity: $a^2 - b^2 = (a+b)(a-b)$
    a. Difference of two squares0
    b. Thing
    c. Undefined
    d. Undefined

63. In mathematics, a matrix can be thought of as each row or _____ being a vector. Hence, a space formed by row vectors or _____ vectors are said to be a row space or a _____ space.
    a. Column0
    b. Concept
    c. Undefined
    d. Undefined

64. In mathematics, a _____ is a particular kind of polynomial, having just one term.
    a. Monomial0
    b. Thing
    c. Undefined
    d. Undefined

65. In mathematics, a _____ is an expression that is constructed from one or more variables and constants, using only the operations of addition, subtraction, multiplication, and constant positive whole number exponents. is a _____. Note in particular that division by an expression containing a variable is not in general allowed in polynomials. [1]
    a. Thing
    b. Polynomial0
    c. Undefined
    d. Undefined

66. In mathematics, the _____ divisor of two non-zero integers, is the largest positive integer that divides both numbers without remainder.
    a. Thing
    b. Greatest common0
    c. Undefined
    d. Undefined

67. In Math the greates common divisor sometimes known as the _____ of two non- zero integers.
    a. Greatest common factor0
    b. Thing
    c. Undefined
    d. Undefined

68. In mathematics, a _____ can mean either an element of the set {1, 2, 3, ...} (i.e the positive integers) or an element of the set {0, 1, 2, 3, ...} (i.e. the non-negative integers).
    a. Concept
    b. Whole number0
    c. Undefined
    d. Undefined

69. _____ is the largest positive integer that divides both numbers without remainder.
    a. Common Factor0
    b. Thing
    c. Undefined
    d. Undefined

Chapter 7. Rational Exponents and Roots

70. In mathematics, _____ is the decomposition of an object into a product of other objects, or factors, which when multiplied together give the original.
    a. Factoring0
    b. Thing
    c. Undefined
    d. Undefined

71. A _____ is a polynomial consisting of three terms; in other words, it is the sum of three monomials.
    a. Trinomial0
    b. Thing
    c. Undefined
    d. Undefined

72. A _____ is a negotiable instrument instructing a financial institution to pay a specific amount of a specific currency from a specific demand account held in the maker/depositor's name with that institution. Both the maker and payee may be natural persons or legal entities.
    a. Check0
    b. Thing
    c. Undefined
    d. Undefined

73. In mathematics, factorization (British English: factorisation) or factoring is the decomposition of an object (for example, a number, a polynomial, or a matrix) into a product of other objects, or _____, which when multiplied together give the original.
    a. Factors0
    b. Thing
    c. Undefined
    d. Undefined

74. A _____ is a numeral used to indicate a count. The most common use of the word today is to name the part of a fraction that tells the number or count of equal parts.
    a. Thing
    b. Numerator0
    c. Undefined
    d. Undefined

75. Equivalence is the condition of being _____ or essentially equal.
    a. Equivalent0
    b. Thing
    c. Undefined
    d. Undefined

76. A _____ is the part of a fraction that tells how many equal parts make up a whole, and which is used in the name of the fraction: "halves", "thirds", "fourths" or "quarters", "fifths" and so on.
    a. Concept
    b. Denominator0
    c. Undefined
    d. Undefined

77. _____ or investing is a term with several closely-related meanings in business management, finance and economics, related to saving or deferring consumption.
    a. Investment0
    b. Thing
    c. Undefined
    d. Undefined

78. A _____ are accounts maintained by commercial banks, savings and loan associations, credit unions, and mutual savings banks that pay interest but can not be used directly as money by, for example, writing a cheque.
    a. Thing
    b. Savings account0
    c. Undefined
    d. Undefined

79. A _____ is a function that assigns a number to subsets of a given set.

Chapter 7. Rational Exponents and Roots

a. Thing
b. Measure0
c. Undefined
d. Undefined

80. Initial objects are also called _____, and terminal objects are also called final.
    a. Coterminal0
    b. Thing
    c. Undefined
    d. Undefined

81. In mathematics and the mathematical sciences, a _____ is a fixed, but possibly unspecified, value. This is in contrast to a variable, which is not fixed.
    a. Thing
    b. Constant0
    c. Undefined
    d. Undefined

82. A _____ is an individual or household that purchases and uses goods and services generated within the economy.
    a. Thing
    b. Consumer0
    c. Undefined
    d. Undefined

83. In arithmetic, _____ is a procedure for calculating the division of one integer, called the dividend, by another integer called the divisor, to produce a result called the quotient.
    a. Thing
    b. Long division0
    c. Undefined
    d. Undefined

84. In physics, an _____ is the path that an object makes around another object while under the influence of a source of centripetal force, such as gravity.
    a. Thing
    b. Orbit0
    c. Undefined
    d. Undefined

85. In business, particularly accounting, a _____ is the time intervals that the accounts, statement, payments, or other calculations cover.
    a. Period0
    b. Thing
    c. Undefined
    d. Undefined

86. A _____, as defined by the International Astronomical Union, is a celestial body orbiting a star or stellar remnant that is massive enough to be rounded by its own gravity, not massive enough to cause thermonuclear fusion in its core, and has cleared its neighboring region of planetesimals.
    a. Planet0
    b. Thing
    c. Undefined
    d. Undefined

87. Kepler's laws of _____ are his primary contributions to astronomy/astrophysics. Kepler, a German mathematician, studied the observations of the legendarily precise Danish astronomer Tycho Brahe, and found around 1605 that these observations followed three relatively simple mathematical laws.
    a. Thing
    b. Planetary motion0
    c. Undefined
    d. Undefined

Chapter 7. Rational Exponents and Roots

88. The _____ are the only integral domain whose positive elements are well-ordered, and in which order is preserved by addition. Like the natural numbers, the _____ form a countably infinite set. The set of all _____ is usually denoted in mathematics by a boldface Z .
   a. Integers0
   b. Thing
   c. Undefined
   d. Undefined

89. In mathematics, a _____ is the end result of a division problem. It can also be expressed as the number of times the divisor divides into the dividend.
   a. Quotient0
   b. Thing
   c. Undefined
   d. Undefined

90. _____ are of a number n in its third power-the result of multiplying it by itself three times.
   a. Thing
   b. Cubes0
   c. Undefined
   d. Undefined

91. A _____ is a number which is the cube of an integer.
   a. Perfect cube0
   b. Thing
   c. Undefined
   d. Undefined

92. The term _____ can refer to an integer which is the square of some other integer, or an algebraic expression that can be factored as the square of some other expression.
   a. Thing
   b. Perfect square0
   c. Undefined
   d. Undefined

93. _____ is a kind of property which exists as magnitude or multitude. It is among the basic classes of things along with quality, substance, change, and relation.
   a. Amount0
   b. Thing
   c. Undefined
   d. Undefined

94. _____, or Rationalisation in mathematics is the process of removing a square root or imaginary number from the denominator of a fraction.
   a. Thing
   b. Rationalizing0
   c. Undefined
   d. Undefined

95. In mathematics, the _____ (or modulus) of a real number is its numerical value without regard to its sign.
   a. Absolute value0
   b. Thing
   c. Undefined
   d. Undefined

96. A _____ is a part of a line that is bounded by two end points, and contains every point on the line between its end points.
   a. Line segment0
   b. Thing
   c. Undefined
   d. Undefined

97. In geometry and trigonometry, a _____ is defined as an angle between two straight intersecting lines of ninety degrees, or one-quarter of a circle.

Chapter 7. Rational Exponents and Roots

   a. Thing
   c. Undefined
   b. Right angle0
   d. Undefined

98. A _____ is a deliberate process for transforming one or more inputs into one or more results.
   a. Calculation0
   c. Undefined
   b. Thing
   d. Undefined

99. A _____ is a simplified and structured visual representation of concepts, ideas, constructions, relations, statistical data, anatomy etc used in all aspects of human activities to visualize and clarify the topic.
   a. Thing
   c. Undefined
   b. Diagram0
   d. Undefined

100. The mathematical concept of a _____ expresses the intuitive idea of deterministic dependence between two quantities, one of which is viewed as primary and the other as secondary. A _____ then is a way to associate a unique output for each input of a specified type, for example, a real number or an element of a given set.
   a. Function0
   c. Undefined
   b. Thing
   d. Undefined

101. In mathematics, a _____ is an ordered list of objects. Like a set, it contains members, also called elements or terms, and the number of terms is called the length of the _____. Unlike a set, order matters, and the exact same elements can appear multiple times at different positions in the _____.
   a. Sequence0
   c. Undefined
   b. Thing
   d. Undefined

102. In colloquial usage, a _____ is "a rough or fragmented geometric shape that can be subdivided in parts, each of which is, at least approximately, a reduced-size copy of the whole."
   a. Fractal0
   c. Undefined
   b. Concept
   d. Undefined

103. The _____ of a solid object is the three-dimensional concept of how much space it occupies, often quantified numerically.
   a. Thing
   c. Undefined
   b. Volume0
   d. Undefined

104. In mathematics, a _____ is the set of all points in three-dimensional space (R^3) which are at distance r from a fixed point of that space, where r is a positive real number called the radius of the _____. The fixed point is called the center or centre, and is not part of the _____ itself.
   a. Thing
   c. Undefined
   b. Sphere0
   d. Undefined

105. In mathematics, a _____ number (or a _____) is a natural number that has exactly two (distinct) natural number divisors, which are 1 and the _____ number itself.
   a. Thing
   c. Undefined
   b. Prime0
   d. Undefined

Chapter 7. Rational Exponents and Roots

106. The _____ of a positive integer are the prime numbers that divide into that integer exactly, without leaving a remainder. The process of finding these numbers is called integer factorization, or prime factorization.
   a. Prime factor0
   b. Thing
   c. Undefined
   d. Undefined

107. In geometry, an _____ polygon is a polygon which has all sides of the same length.
   a. Thing
   b. Equilateral0
   c. Undefined
   d. Undefined

108. An _____ is a triangle in which all sides are of equal length.
   a. Thing
   b. Equilateral triangle0
   c. Undefined
   d. Undefined

109. In mathematics, _____ is an elementary arithmetic operation. When one of the numbers is a whole number, _____ is the repeated sum of the other number.
   a. Thing
   b. Multiplication0
   c. Undefined
   d. Undefined

110. In abstract algebra, _____ consists of sets with binary operations that satisfy certain axioms.
   a. Grouping0
   b. Thing
   c. Undefined
   d. Undefined

111. A _____ signifies a point or points of probability on a subject e.g., the _____ of creativity, which allows for the formation of rule or norm or law by interpretation of the phenomena events that can be created.
   a. Thing
   b. Principle0
   c. Undefined
   d. Undefined

112. In algebra, a _____ is a binomial formed by taking the opposite of the second term of a binomial.
   a. Thing
   b. Conjugate0
   c. Undefined
   d. Undefined

113. Two mathematical objects are equal if and only if they are precisely the same in every way. This defines a binary relation, _____, denoted by the sign of _____ "=" in such a way that the statement "x = y" means that x and y are equal.
   a. Thing
   b. Equality0
   c. Undefined
   d. Undefined

114. _____ variables are variables other than the independent variable that may bear any effect on the behavior of the subject being studied.
   a. Thing
   b. Extraneous0
   c. Undefined
   d. Undefined

115. In mathematics, a _____ is a polynomial equation of the second degree. The general form is $ax^2 + bx + c = 0$.
   a. Quadratic equation0
   b. Thing
   c. Undefined
   d. Undefined

Chapter 7. Rational Exponents and Roots

116. _____ is a notation for writing numbers that is often used by scientists and mathematicians to make it easier to write large and small numbers.
   a. Scientific notation0
   b. Thing
   c. Undefined
   d. Undefined

117. A _____ consists of one quarter of the coordinate plane.
   a. Quadrant0
   b. Thing
   c. Undefined
   d. Undefined

118. A _____ is an object that is attached to a pivot point so that it can swing freely.
   a. Thing
   b. Pendulum0
   c. Undefined
   d. Undefined

119. Johann Carl Friedrich Gauss or _____ was a German mathematician and scientist of profound genius who contributed significantly to many fields, including number theory, analysis, differential geometry, geodesy, magnetism, astronomy, and optics.
   a. Person
   b. Carl Gauss0
   c. Undefined
   d. Undefined

120. In mathematics, a _____ is a number in the form of a + bi where a and b are real numbers, and i is the imaginary unit, with the property i 2 = −1. The real number a is called the real part of the _____, and the real number b is the imaginary part.
   a. Complex number0
   b. Thing
   c. Undefined
   d. Undefined

121. A _____ decimal is a number whose decimal representation eventually becomes periodic (i.e. the same number sequence _____ indefinitely).
   a. Thing
   b. Repeating0
   c. Undefined
   d. Undefined

122. In mathematics, the _____ of a complex number z, is the first element of the ordered pair of real numbers representing z, i.e. if z = (x,y), or equivalently, z = x + iy, then the _____ of z is x. It is denoted by Re{z} . The complex function which maps z to the _____ of z is not holomorphic.
   a. Thing
   b. Real part0
   c. Undefined
   d. Undefined

123. In mathematics, an _____ number is a complex number whose square is a negative real number. They were defined in 1572 by Rafael Bombelli.
   a. Imaginary0
   b. Thing
   c. Undefined
   d. Undefined

124. In mathematics, the _____ of a complex number z, is the second element of the ordered pair of real numbers representing z, i.e. if z = (x,y), or equivalently, z = x + iy, then the _____ of z is y.
   a. Imaginary part0
   b. Thing
   c. Undefined
   d. Undefined

Chapter 7. Rational Exponents and Roots

125. _____ is the mathematical action of repeatedly adding or subtracting one, usually to find out how many objects there are or to set aside a desired number of objects.
  a. Counting0
  b. Thing
  c. Undefined
  d. Undefined

126. In mathematics, an _____ is a complex number whose square is a negative real number. They were defined in 1572 by Rafael Bombelli.
  a. Imaginary number0
  b. Thing
  c. Undefined
  d. Undefined

127. In mathematics, an _____ number is any real number that is not a rational number- that is, it is a number which cannot be expressed as a fraction m/n, where m and n are integers.
  a. Thing
  b. Irrational0
  c. Undefined
  d. Undefined

128. In mathematics, the multiplicative inverse of a number x, denoted 1/x or x^{-1}, is the number which, when multiplied by x, yields 1. The multiplicative inverse of x is also called the _____ of x.
  a. Thing
  b. Reciprocal0
  c. Undefined
  d. Undefined

129. In mathematics, the additive inverse, or _____ of a number n is the number that, when added to n, yields zero. The additive inverse of n is denoted −n. For example, 7 is −7, because 7 + (−7) = 0, and the additive inverse of −0.3 is 0.3, because −0.3 + 0.3 = 0.
  a. Thing
  b. Opposite0
  c. Undefined
  d. Undefined

130. In mathematics, the _____ of a number n is the number that, when added to n, yields zero. The _____ of n is denoted −n. For example, 7 is −7, because 7 + (−7) = 0, and the _____ of −0.3 is 0.3, because −0.3 + 0.3 = 0.
  a. Thing
  b. Additive inverse0
  c. Undefined
  d. Undefined

131. _____ is the technique and science of accurately determining the terrestrial or three-dimensional space position of points and the distances and angles between them.
  a. Surveying0
  b. Thing
  c. Undefined
  d. Undefined

132. Compass and straightedge or ruler-and-compass _____ is the _____ of lengths or angles using only an idealized ruler and compass.
  a. Thing
  b. Construction0
  c. Undefined
  d. Undefined

133. In mathematics, an _____ is a statement about the relative size or order of two objects.
  a. Inequality0
  b. Thing
  c. Undefined
  d. Undefined

Chapter 7. Rational Exponents and Roots

134. A _____ is a set of numbers that designate location in a given reference system, such as x,y in a planar _____ system or an x,y,z in a three-dimensional _____ system.
   a. Coordinate0
   b. Thing
   c. Undefined
   d. Undefined

135. In mathematics and its applications, a _____ is a system for assigning an n-tuple of numbers or scalars to each point in an n-dimensional space.
   a. Concept
   b. Coordinate system0
   c. Undefined
   d. Undefined

136. _____ is often used to describe the measurement of the steepness, incline, gradient, or grade of a straight line. The _____ is defined as the ratio of the "rise" divided by the "run" between two points on a line, or in other words, the ratio of the altitude change to the horizontal distance between any two points on the line.
   a. Slope0
   b. Thing
   c. Undefined
   d. Undefined

137. _____ are a measure of time.
   a. Thing
   b. Minutes0
   c. Undefined
   d. Undefined

138. In mathematics, an _____ is any real number that is not a rational number ¡ª that is, it is a number which cannot be expressed as m/n, where m and n are integers.
   a. Irrational number0
   b. Thing
   c. Undefined
   d. Undefined

139. In mathematics, _____ are any real number that is not a rational number ¡ª that is, it is a number which cannot be expressed as m/n, where m and n are integers.
   a. Irrational numbers0
   b. Thing
   c. Undefined
   d. Undefined

140. In geometry, two lines or planes if one falls on the other in such a way as to create congruent adjacent angles. The term may be used as a noun or adjective. Thus, referring to Figure 1, the line AB is the _____ to CD through the point B.
   a. Thing
   b. Perpendicular0
   c. Undefined
   d. Undefined

141. A _____ is an instrument used in geometry technical drawing and engineering/building to measure distances and/or to rule straight lines.
   a. Ruler0
   b. Thing
   c. Undefined
   d. Undefined

142. The _____ of a right triangle is the triangle's longest side; the side opposite the right angle.
   a. Hypotenuse0
   b. Thing
   c. Undefined
   d. Undefined

143. _____ was an Italian linguist, mathematician, and philosopher.

Chapter 7. Rational Exponents and Roots

a. Thing
b. Maria Agnesi0
c. Undefined
d. Undefined

144. In Euclidean geometry, a _____ is moving every point a constant distance in a specified direction.
a. Translation0
b. Concept
c. Undefined
d. Undefined

145. In mathematics, the _____, sometimes called the witch of Maria Agnesi is the curve defined as follows. Starting with a fixed circle, a point O on the circle is chosen. For any other point A on the circle, the secant line OA is drawn. The point M is diametrically opposite O. The line OA intersects the tangent at M at the point N. The line parallel to OM through N, and the line perpedicular to OM through A intersect at P. As the point A is varied, the path of P is the witch.
a. Witch of Agnesi0
b. Thing
c. Undefined
d. Undefined

146. In mathematics, a _____ is a collection of points which share a property.
a. Locus0
b. Thing
c. Undefined
d. Undefined

Chapter 8. Quadratic Functions

1. _____ is the transport of people on a trip/journey or the process or time involved in a person or object moving from one location to another.
   a. Thing
   b. Travel0
   c. Undefined
   d. Undefined

2. In topology and related areas of mathematics a _____ or Moore-Smith sequence is a generalization of a sequence, intended to unify the various notions of limit and generalize them to arbitrary topological spaces.
   a. Net0
   b. Thing
   c. Undefined
   d. Undefined

3. A _____ is one of the basic shapes of geometry: a polygon with three vertices and three sides which are straight line segments.
   a. Triangle0
   b. Thing
   c. Undefined
   d. Undefined

4. A _____ is an abstract model that uses mathematical language to describe the behavior of a system. Eykhoff defined a _____ as 'a representation of the essential aspects of an existing system which presents knowledge of that system in usable form'.
   a. Mathematical model0
   b. Thing
   c. Undefined
   d. Undefined

5. _____ has one 90° internal angle a right angle.
   a. Right triangle0
   b. Thing
   c. Undefined
   d. Undefined

6. In mathematics, a _____ is a polynomial equation of the second degree. The general form is $ax^2 + bx + c = 0$.
   a. Thing
   b. Quadratic equation0
   c. Undefined
   d. Undefined

7. In plane geometry, a _____ is a polygon with four equal sides, four right angles, and parallel opposite sides. In algebra, the _____ of a number is that number multiplied by itself.
   a. Thing
   b. Square0
   c. Undefined
   d. Undefined

8. _____ is a technique used in algebra to solve quadratic equations, in analytic geometry for determining the shapes of graphs, and in calculus for computing integrals, including, but hardly limited to, the integrals that define Laplace transforms. The essential objective is to reduce a quadratic polynomial in a variable in an equation or expression to a squared polynomial of linear order. This can reduce an equation or integral to one that is more easily solved or evaluated.
   a. Completing the square0
   b. Thing
   c. Undefined
   d. Undefined

9. In mathematics, a _____ of a number x is a number r such that $r^2 = x$, or in words, a number r whose square (the result of multiplying the number by itself) is x.
   a. Square root0
   b. Thing
   c. Undefined
   d. Undefined

Chapter 8. Quadratic Functions

10. In mathematics, a _____ of a complex-valued function f is a member x of the domain of f such that f(x) vanishes at x, that is, x : f (x) = 0.
    a. Thing
    b. Root0
    c. Undefined
    d. Undefined

11. In mathematics, a _____ may be described informally as a number that can be given by an infinite decimal representation.
    a. Real number0
    b. Thing
    c. Undefined
    d. Undefined

12. In mathematics, a _____ is a statement that can be proved on the basis of explicitly stated or previously agreed assumptions.
    a. Thing
    b. Theorem0
    c. Undefined
    d. Undefined

13. Mathematical _____ is used to represent ideas.
    a. Thing
    b. Notation0
    c. Undefined
    d. Undefined

14. An _____ is a combination of numbers, operators, grouping symbols and/or free variables and bound variables arranged in a meaningful way which can be evaluated..
    a. Thing
    b. Expression0
    c. Undefined
    d. Undefined

15. The plus and _____ signs are mathematical symbols used to represent the notions of positive and negative as well as the operations of addition and subtraction.
    a. Minus0
    b. Thing
    c. Undefined
    d. Undefined

16. A _____ is a set of possible values that a variable can take on in order to satisfy a given set of conditions, which may include equations and inequalities.
    a. Thing
    b. Solution set0
    c. Undefined
    d. Undefined

17. In common philosophical language, a proposition or _____, is the content of an assertion, that is, it is true-or-false and defined by the meaning of a particular piece of language.
    a. Statement0
    b. Concept
    c. Undefined
    d. Undefined

18. In mathematics, _____ is the decomposition of an object into a product of other objects, or factors, which when multiplied together give the original.
    a. Factoring0
    b. Thing
    c. Undefined
    d. Undefined

19. _____ is a notation for writing numbers that is often used by scientists and mathematicians to make it easier to write large and small numbers.

Chapter 8. Quadratic Functions

a. Thing
c. Undefined

b. Scientific notation0
d. Undefined

20. A _____ is a symbolic representation denoting a quantity or expression. It often represents an "unknown" quantity that has the potential to change.

a. Thing
c. Undefined

b. Variable0
d. Undefined

21. In mathematics, factorization (British English: factorisation) or factoring is the decomposition of an object (for example, a number, a polynomial, or a matrix) into a product of other objects, or _____, which when multiplied together give the original.

a. Thing
c. Undefined

b. Factors0
d. Undefined

22. The mathematical concept of a _____ expresses the intuitive idea of deterministic dependence between two quantities, one of which is viewed as primary and the other as secondary. A _____ then is a way to associate a unique output for each input of a specified type, for example, a real number or an element of a given set.

a. Thing
c. Undefined

b. Function0
d. Undefined

23. In mathematics, a _____ is a constant multiplicative factor of a certain object. The object can be such things as a variable, a vector, a function, etc. For example, the _____ of $9x^2$ is 9.

a. Thing
c. Undefined

b. Coefficient0
d. Undefined

24. In mathematics and the mathematical sciences, a _____ is a fixed, but possibly unspecified, value. This is in contrast to a variable, which is not fixed.

a. Constant0
c. Undefined

b. Thing
d. Undefined

25. _____ is a fixed, but possibly unspecified, value. This is in contrast to a variable, which is not fixed.

a. Constant term0
c. Undefined

b. Thing
d. Undefined

26. The term _____ can refer to an integer which is the square of some other integer, or an algebraic expression that can be factored as the square of some other expression.

a. Thing
c. Undefined

b. Perfect square0
d. Undefined

27. _____ is the symbol used to indicate the nth root of a number

a. Thing
c. Undefined

b. Radical0
d. Undefined

28. The word _____ comes from the Latin word linearis, which means created by lines.

Chapter 8. Quadratic Functions

    a. Thing
    b. Linear0
    c. Undefined
    d. Undefined

29. In elementary algebra, a _____ is a polynomial with two terms: the sum of two monomials. It is the simplest kind of polynomial except for a monomial.
    a. Thing
    b. Binomial0
    c. Undefined
    d. Undefined

30. _____ is a relation in Euclidean geometry among the three sides of a right triangle.
    a. Thing
    b. Pythagorean Theorem0
    c. Undefined
    d. Undefined

31. In astronomy, geography, geometry and related sciences and contexts, a plane is said to be _____ at a given point if it is locally perpendicular to the gradient of the gravity field, i.e., with the direction of the gravitational force at that point.
    a. Horizontal0
    b. Thing
    c. Undefined
    d. Undefined

32. The _____ of a right triangle is the triangle's longest side; the side opposite the right angle.
    a. Thing
    b. Hypotenuse0
    c. Undefined
    d. Undefined

33. _____ are flexible, elastic objects used to store mechanical energy.
    a. Thing
    b. Springs0
    c. Undefined
    d. Undefined

34. A _____ is a special kind of ratio, indicating a relationship between two measurements with different units, such as miles to gallons or cents to pounds.
    a. Rate0
    b. Thing
    c. Undefined
    d. Undefined

35. _____ is the fee paid on borrowed money.
    a. Interest0
    b. Thing
    c. Undefined
    d. Undefined

36. An _____ is the fee paid on borrow money.
    a. Concept
    b. Interest rate0
    c. Undefined
    d. Undefined

37. A _____ is the part of a fraction that tells how many equal parts make up a whole, and which is used in the name of the fraction: "halves", "thirds", "fourths" or "quarters", "fifths" and so on.
    a. Denominator0
    b. Concept
    c. Undefined
    d. Undefined

38. A quadratic equation with real solutions, called roots, which may be real or complex, is given by the _____: $x = \frac{-b \pm \sqrt{b^2 - 4ac}}{}$

Chapter 8. Quadratic Functions

    a. Thing
    b. Quadratic formula0
    c. Undefined
    d. Undefined

39. In mathematics, a _____ is a demonstration that, assuming certain axioms, some statement is necessarily true.
    a. Thing
    b. Proof0
    c. Undefined
    d. Undefined

40. The _____ rule, also known as a slipstick, is a mechanical analog computer, consisting of at least two finely divided scales, most often a fixed outer pair and a movable inner one, with a sliding window called the cursor.
    a. Slide0
    b. Thing
    c. Undefined
    d. Undefined

41. _____ or arithmetics is the oldest and most elementary branch of mathematics, used by almost everyone, for tasks ranging from simple daily counting to advanced science and business calculations.
    a. Arithmetic0
    b. Thing
    c. Undefined
    d. Undefined

42. In mathematics, a _____ number is a number which can be expressed as a ratio of two integers. Non-integer _____ numbers (commonly called fractions) are usually written as the vulgar fraction a / b, where b is not zero.
    a. Rational0
    b. Thing
    c. Undefined
    d. Undefined

43. The _____, the average in everyday English, which is also called the arithmetic _____ (and is distinguished from the geometric _____ or harmonic _____). The average is also called the sample _____. The expected value of a random variable, which is also called the population _____.
    a. Mean0
    b. Thing
    c. Undefined
    d. Undefined

44. A _____ is a numeral used to indicate a count. The most common use of the word today is to name the part of a fraction that tells the number or count of equal parts.
    a. Numerator0
    b. Thing
    c. Undefined
    d. Undefined

45. A _____ is a three-dimensional solid object bounded by six square faces, facets, or sides, with three meeting at each vertex.
    a. Thing
    b. Cube0
    c. Undefined
    d. Undefined

46. A _____ of a number is a number a such that $a^3 = x$.
    a. Cube root0
    b. Thing
    c. Undefined
    d. Undefined

47. A _____ is a number that is less than zero.
    a. Negative number0
    b. Thing
    c. Undefined
    d. Undefined

Chapter 8. Quadratic Functions

48. _____, from Latin meaning "to make progress", is defined in two different ways. Pure economic _____ is the increase in wealth that an investor has from making an investment, taking into consideration all costs associated with that investment including the opportunity cost of capital.
   a. Thing
   b. Profit0
   c. Undefined
   d. Undefined

49. _____ is a business term for the amount of money that a company receives from its activities in a given period, mostly from sales of products and/or services to customers
   a. Thing
   b. Revenue0
   c. Undefined
   d. Undefined

50. In mathematics, the additive inverse, or _____ of a number n is the number that, when added to n, yields zero. The additive inverse of n is denoted −n. For example, 7 is −7, because 7 + (−7) = 0, and the additive inverse of −0.3 is 0.3, because −0.3 + 0.3 = 0.
   a. Opposite0
   b. Thing
   c. Undefined
   d. Undefined

51. In mathematics, a _____ is an expression that is constructed from one or more variables and constants, using only the operations of addition, subtraction, multiplication, and constant positive whole number exponents. is a _____. Note in particular that division by an expression containing a variable is not in general allowed in polynomials. [1]
   a. Polynomial0
   b. Thing
   c. Undefined
   d. Undefined

52. In mathematics, the _____ of a number n is the number that, when added to n, yields zero. The _____ of n is denoted −n. For example, 7 is −7, because 7 + (−7) = 0, and the _____ of −0.3 is 0.3, because −0.3 + 0.3 = 0.
   a. Additive inverse0
   b. Thing
   c. Undefined
   d. Undefined

53. _____ are the basic objects of study in graph theory. Informally speaking, a graph is a set of objects called points, nodes, or vertices connected by links called lines or edges.
   a. Graphs0
   b. Thing
   c. Undefined
   d. Undefined

54. A _____ is a polynomial function of the form $f(x) = ax^2 + bx + c$, where a, b, c are real numbers and a , 0.
   a. Event
   b. Quadratic function0
   c. Undefined
   d. Undefined

55. _____ of an object is its speed in a particular direction.
   a. Velocity0
   b. Thing
   c. Undefined
   d. Undefined

56. Initial objects are also called _____, and terminal objects are also called final.
   a. Coterminal0
   b. Thing
   c. Undefined
   d. Undefined

57. A _____ is a function that assigns a number to subsets of a given set.

a. Thing
b. Measure0
c. Undefined
d. Undefined

58. The metre (or _____, see spelling differences) is a measure of length. It is the basic unit of length in the metric system and in the International System of Units (SI), used around the world for general and scientific purposes.
   a. Concept
   b. Meter0
   c. Undefined
   d. Undefined

59. A _____ is a simplified and structured visual representation of concepts, ideas, constructions, relations, statistical data, anatomy etc used in all aspects of human activities to visualize and clarify the topic.
   a. Thing
   b. Diagram0
   c. Undefined
   d. Undefined

60. In geometry, a _____ is defined as a quadrilateral where all four of its angles are right angles.
   a. Thing
   b. Rectangle0
   c. Undefined
   d. Undefined

61. _____ is the distance around a given two-dimensional object. As a general rule, the _____ of a polygon can always be calculated by adding all the length of the sides together. So, the formula for triangles is P = a + b + c, where a, b and c stand for each side of it. For quadrilaterals the equation is P = a + b + c + d. For equilateral polygons, P = na, where n is the number of sides and a is the side length.
   a. Thing
   b. Perimeter0
   c. Undefined
   d. Undefined

62. In sociology and biology a _____ is the collection of people or organisms of a particular species living in a given geographic area or space, usually measured by a census.
   a. Thing
   b. Population0
   c. Undefined
   d. Undefined

63. A _____ is a statement or claimt that a particular event will occur in the future in more certain terms than a forecast.
   a. Thing
   b. Prediction0
   c. Undefined
   d. Undefined

64. _____ of a polynomial with real or complex coefficients is a certain expression in the coefficients of the polynomial which is equal to zero if and only if the polynomial has a multiple root i.e. a root with multiplicity greater than one in the complex numbers.
   a. Thing
   b. Discriminant0
   c. Undefined
   d. Undefined

65. The _____ of a member of a multiset is how many memberships in the multiset it has.
   a. Thing
   b. Multiplicity0
   c. Undefined
   d. Undefined

66. In mathematics, a _____ is the result of multiplying, or an expression that identifies factors to be multiplied.

a. Thing
b. Product0
c. Undefined
d. Undefined

67. In mathematics, _____ is an elementary arithmetic operation. When one of the numbers is a whole number, _____ is the repeated sum of the other number.
    a. Thing
    b. Multiplication0
    c. Undefined
    d. Undefined

68. _____ is a branch of mathematics concerning the study of structure, relation and quantity.
    a. Algebra0
    b. Concept
    c. Undefined
    d. Undefined

69. In linear algebra, the _____ of an n-by-n square matrix A is defined to be the sum of the elements on the main diagonal of A,
    a. Thing
    b. Trace0
    c. Undefined
    d. Undefined

70. A _____ is a set of numbers that designate location in a given reference system, such as x,y in a planar _____ system or an x,y,z in a three-dimensional _____ system.
    a. Coordinate0
    b. Thing
    c. Undefined
    d. Undefined

71. In mathematics, the concept of a _____ tries to capture the intuitive idea of a geometrical one-dimensional and continuous object. A simple example is the circle.
    a. Thing
    b. Curve0
    c. Undefined
    d. Undefined

72. In mathematics, _____ are the intuitive idea of a geometrical one-dimensional and continuous object.
    a. Thing
    b. Curves0
    c. Undefined
    d. Undefined

73. In geographic information systems, a _____ comprises an entity with a geographic location, typically determined by points, arcs, or polygons. Carriageways and cadastres exemplify _____ data.
    a. Thing
    b. Feature0
    c. Undefined
    d. Undefined

74. In mathematics, the _____ of two sets A and B is the set that contains all elements of A that also belong to B (or equivalently, all elements of B that also belong to A), but no other elements.
    a. Thing
    b. Intersection0
    c. Undefined
    d. Undefined

75. Equivalence is the condition of being _____ or essentially equal.
    a. Equivalent0
    b. Thing
    c. Undefined
    d. Undefined

76. _____ is the process of reducing the number of significant digits in a number.

a. Concept
b. Rounding0
c. Undefined
d. Undefined

77. _____ variables are variables other than the independent variable that may bear any effect on the behavior of the subject being studied.
   a. Thing
   b. Extraneous0
   c. Undefined
   d. Undefined

78. A _____ is a negotiable instrument instructing a financial institution to pay a specific amount of a specific currency from a specific demand account held in the maker/depositor's name with that institution. Both the maker and payee may be natural persons or legal entities.
   a. Check0
   b. Thing
   c. Undefined
   d. Undefined

79. The _____ of measurement are a globally standardized and modernized form of the metric system.
   a. Units0
   b. Thing
   c. Undefined
   d. Undefined

80. The _____ is a number often encountered when taking the ratios of distances in simple geometric figures. It is approximately 1.6180339887.
   a. Golden ratio0
   b. Thing
   c. Undefined
   d. Undefined

81. A _____ is a rectangle whose side lengths are in the golden ratio, 1:, that is, approximately 1:1.618.
   a. Golden rectangle0
   b. Thing
   c. Undefined
   d. Undefined

82. A _____ is a quantity that denotes the proportional amount or magnitude of one quantity relative to another.
   a. Thing
   b. Ratio0
   c. Undefined
   d. Undefined

83. _____, also known as _____ of Alexandria, was a Greek mathematician. His Elements is the most successful textbook in the history of mathematics. In it, the principles of geometry are deduced from a small set of axioms. His method of proving mathematical theorems by logical reasoning from accepted first principles remains the backbone of mathematics and is responsible for the field's characteristic rigor
   a. Euclid0
   b. Person
   c. Undefined
   d. Undefined

84. In geometry, a line _____ is a part of a line that is bounded by two end points, and contains every point on the line between its end points.
   a. Concept
   b. Segment0
   c. Undefined
   d. Undefined

85. A _____ is a part of a line that is bounded by two end points, and contains every point on the line between its end points.

Chapter 8. Quadratic Functions

    a. Line segment0
    b. Thing
    c. Undefined
    d. Undefined

86. In mathematics, the _____ is a conic section generated by the intersection of a right circular conical surface and a plane parallel to a generating straight line of that surface. It can also be defined as locus of points in a plane which are equidistant from a given point.
    a. Parabola0
    b. Thing
    c. Undefined
    d. Undefined

87. An _____ is a straight line around which a geometric figure can be rotated.
    a. Thing
    b. Axis0
    c. Undefined
    d. Undefined

88. An _____ is a collection of two not necessarily distinct objects, one of which is distinguished as the first coordinate and the other as the second coordinate.
    a. Thing
    b. Ordered pair0
    c. Undefined
    d. Undefined

89. In mathematics, the conjugate _____ or adjoint matrix of an m-by-n matrix A with complex entries is the n-by-m matrix A* obtained from A by taking the transpose and then taking the complex conjugate of each entry.
    a. Pairs0
    b. Thing
    c. Undefined
    d. Undefined

90. In geometry, a _____ is a special kind of point, usually a corner of a polygon, polyhedron, or higher dimensional polytope. In the geometry of curves a _____ is a point of where the first derivative of curvature is zero. In graph theory, a _____ is the fundamental unit out of which graphs are formed
    a. Thing
    b. Vertex0
    c. Undefined
    d. Undefined

91. _____, either of the curved-bracket punctuation marks that together make a set of _____
    a. Thing
    b. Parentheses0
    c. Undefined
    d. Undefined

92. In mathematics, an _____ number is any real number that is not a rational number- that is, it is a number which cannot be expressed as a fraction m/n, where m and n are integers.
    a. Thing
    b. Irrational0
    c. Undefined
    d. Undefined

93. In mathematics, a _____ is a number in the form of a + bi where a and b are real numbers, and i is the imaginary unit, with the property i 2 = −1. The real number a is called the real part of the _____, and the real number b is the imaginary part.
    a. Complex number0
    b. Thing
    c. Undefined
    d. Undefined

94. A _____ consists of one quarter of the coordinate plane.

a. Thing
b. Quadrant0
c. Undefined
d. Undefined

95. In mathematics and its applications, a _____ is a system for assigning an n-tuple of numbers or scalars to each point in an n-dimensional space.
a. Concept
b. Coordinate system0
c. Undefined
d. Undefined

96. In mathematics, the _____ of a coordinate system is the point where the axes of the system intersect.
a. Thing
b. Origin0
c. Undefined
d. Undefined

97. In set theory and other branches of mathematics, the _____ of a collection of sets is the set that contains everything that belongs to any of the sets, but nothing else.
a. Thing
b. Union0
c. Undefined
d. Undefined

98. In mathematics, an _____ is a statement about the relative size or order of two objects.
a. Inequality0
b. Thing
c. Undefined
d. Undefined

99. In geometry, an _____ is a point at which a line segment or ray terminates.
a. Thing
b. Endpoint0
c. Undefined
d. Undefined

100. In a mathematical proof or a syllogism, a _____ is a statement that is the logical consequence of preceding statements.
a. Conclusion0
b. Concept
c. Undefined
d. Undefined

101. A _____ is any object propelled through space by the applicationp of a force.
a. Projectile0
b. Thing
c. Undefined
d. Undefined

102. _____ is the path a moving object follows through space.
a. Thing
b. Projectile motion0
c. Undefined
d. Undefined

103. The _____ of a solid object is the three-dimensional concept of how much space it occupies, often quantified numerically.
a. Volume0
b. Thing
c. Undefined
d. Undefined

Chapter 9. Exponential and Logarithmic Functions

1. The _____, the average in everyday English, which is also called the arithmetic _____ (and is distinguished from the geometric _____ or harmonic _____). The average is also called the sample _____. The expected value of a random variable, which is also called the population _____.
   a. Thing
   b. Mean0
   c. Undefined
   d. Undefined

2. _____ is a kind of property which exists as magnitude or multitude. It is among the basic classes of things along with quality, substance, change, and relation.
   a. Thing
   b. Amount0
   c. Undefined
   d. Undefined

3. _____ is a subset of a population.
   a. Sample0
   b. Thing
   c. Undefined
   d. Undefined

4. Initial objects are also called _____, and terminal objects are also called final.
   a. Coterminal0
   b. Thing
   c. Undefined
   d. Undefined

5. In mathematics, _____ growth occurs when the growth rate of a function is always proportional to the function's current size.
   a. Thing
   b. Exponential0
   c. Undefined
   d. Undefined

6. The mathematical concept of a _____ expresses the intuitive idea of deterministic dependence between two quantities, one of which is viewed as primary and the other as secondary. A _____ then is a way to associate a unique output for each input of a specified type, for example, a real number or an element of a given set.
   a. Thing
   b. Function0
   c. Undefined
   d. Undefined

7. A _____ is 360° or 2δ radians.
   a. Turn0
   b. Thing
   c. Undefined
   d. Undefined

8. _____ are the basic objects of study in graph theory. Informally speaking, a graph is a set of objects called points, nodes, or vertices connected by links called lines or edges.
   a. Thing
   b. Graphs0
   c. Undefined
   d. Undefined

9. _____ is one of the most important functions in mathematics. A function commonly used to study growth and decay
   a. Thing
   b. Exponential function0
   c. Undefined
   d. Undefined

10. Mathematical _____ is used to represent ideas.

Chapter 9. Exponential and Logarithmic Functions

a. Thing
b. Notation0
c. Undefined
d. Undefined

11. In geometry, _____ lines are two lines that share one or more common points.
    a. Intersecting0
    b. Thing
    c. Undefined
    d. Undefined

12. In mathematics, the concept of a _____ tries to capture the intuitive idea of a geometrical one-dimensional and continuous object. A simple example is the circle.
    a. Thing
    b. Curve0
    c. Undefined
    d. Undefined

13. In mathematics, _____ are the intuitive idea of a geometrical one-dimensional and continuous object.
    a. Thing
    b. Curves0
    c. Undefined
    d. Undefined

14. _____ is the fee paid on borrowed money.
    a. Interest0
    b. Thing
    c. Undefined
    d. Undefined

15. A _____ is a special kind of ratio, indicating a relationship between two measurements with different units, such as miles to gallons or cents to pounds.
    a. Rate0
    b. Thing
    c. Undefined
    d. Undefined

16. _____ interest refers to the fact that whenever interest is calculated, it is based not only on the original principal, but also on any unpaid interest that has been added to the principal.
    a. Compound0
    b. Thing
    c. Undefined
    d. Undefined

17. _____ refers to the fact that whenever interest is calculated, it is based not only on the original principal, but also on any unpaid interest that has been added to the principal. The more frequently interest is compounded, the faster the balance grows.
    a. Concept
    b. Compound interest0
    c. Undefined
    d. Undefined

18. An _____ is the fee paid on borrow money.
    a. Concept
    b. Interest rate0
    c. Undefined
    d. Undefined

19. In linear algebra, the _____ of an n-by-n square matrix A is defined to be the sum of the elements on the main diagonal of A,
    a. Thing
    b. Trace0
    c. Undefined
    d. Undefined

Chapter 9. Exponential and Logarithmic Functions

20. In mathematics, an _____ number is any real number that is not a rational number- that is, it is a number which cannot be expressed as a fraction m/n, where m and n are integers.
    a. Irrational0
    b. Thing
    c. Undefined
    d. Undefined

21. _____ is a decrease that follows an exponential function.
    a. Thing
    b. Exponential decay0
    c. Undefined
    d. Undefined

22. In mathematics, _____ occurs when the growth rate of a function is always proportional to the function's current size.
    a. Exponential growth0
    b. Thing
    c. Undefined
    d. Undefined

23. _____ is the level of functional and/or metabolic efficiency of an organism at both the micro level.
    a. Thing
    b. Health0
    c. Undefined
    d. Undefined

24. _____ in the United States have been estimated to reach 15% of the gross domestic product, according to the World Health Report, 2006.
    a. Thing
    b. Health care expenditures0
    c. Undefined
    d. Undefined

25. _____ or investing is a term with several closely-related meanings in business management, finance and economics, related to saving or deferring consumption.
    a. Investment0
    b. Thing
    c. Undefined
    d. Undefined

26. In mathematics, a _____ of a k-place relation $L \subseteq X_1 \times \ldots \times X_k$ is one of the sets X_j, $1 \leq j \leq k$. In the special case where k = 2 and $L \subseteq X_1 \times X_2$ is a function $L : X_1 \to X_2$, it is conventional to refer to X_1 as the _____ of the function and to refer to X_2 as the codomain of the function.
    a. Thing
    b. Domain0
    c. Undefined
    d. Undefined

27. In geometry, a line _____ is a part of a line that is bounded by two end points, and contains every point on the line between its end points.
    a. Segment0
    b. Concept
    c. Undefined
    d. Undefined

28. In botany, _____ are above-ground plant organs specialized for photosynthesis. Their characteristics are typically analyzed by using Fiobonacci's sequences.
    a. Leaves0
    b. Thing
    c. Undefined
    d. Undefined

Chapter 9. Exponential and Logarithmic Functions

29. In mathematics, the additive inverse, or _____ of a number n is the number that, when added to n, yields zero. The additive inverse of n is denoted −n. For example, 7 is −7, because 7 + (−7) = 0, and the additive inverse of −0.3 is 0.3, because −0.3 + 0.3 = 0.
    - a. Opposite0
    - b. Thing
    - c. Undefined
    - d. Undefined

30. In mathematics, the _____ of a number n is the number that, when added to n, yields zero. The _____ of n is denoted −n. For example, 7 is −7, because 7 + (−7) = 0, and the _____ of −0.3 is 0.3, because −0.3 + 0.3 = 0.
    - a. Thing
    - b. Additive inverse0
    - c. Undefined
    - d. Undefined

31. A _____ is a unit of length, usually used to measure distance, in a number of different systems, including Imperial units, United States customary units and Norwegian/Swedish mil. Its size can vary from system to system, but in each is between 1 and 10 kilometers. In contemporary English contexts _____ refers to either:
    - a. Mile0
    - b. Thing
    - c. Undefined
    - d. Undefined

32. _____ element of an element x with respect to a binary operation * with identity element e is an element y such that x * y = y * x = e. In particular,
    - a. Inverse0
    - b. Thing
    - c. Undefined
    - d. Undefined

33. An _____ is a function which does the reverse of a given function.
    - a. Inverse function0
    - b. Thing
    - c. Undefined
    - d. Undefined

34. In mathematics, the _____ of a function is the set of all "output" values produced by that function. Given a function $f: A \to B$, the _____ of f, is defined to be the set $\{x \in B : x = f(a) \text{ for some } a \in A\}$.
    - a. Range0
    - b. Thing
    - c. Undefined
    - d. Undefined

35. An _____ is a collection of two not necessarily distinct objects, one of which is distinguished as the first coordinate and the other as the second coordinate.
    - a. Thing
    - b. Ordered pair0
    - c. Undefined
    - d. Undefined

36. In mathematics, in the field of group theory, a _____ of a group is a quasisimple subnormal subgroup.
    - a. Concept
    - b. Component0
    - c. Undefined
    - d. Undefined

37. In mathematics, the conjugate _____ or adjoint matrix of an m-by-n matrix A with complex entries is the n-by-m matrix A* obtained from A by taking the transpose and then taking the complex conjugate of each entry.
    - a. Pairs0
    - b. Thing
    - c. Undefined
    - d. Undefined

Chapter 9. Exponential and Logarithmic Functions

38. _____ means "constancy", i.e. if something retains a certain feature even after we change a way of looking at it, then it is symmetric.
    a. Thing
    b. Symmetry0
    c. Undefined
    d. Undefined

39. An _____ or member of a set is an object that when collected together make up the set.
    a. Thing
    b. Element0
    c. Undefined
    d. Undefined

40. In mathematics, the _____ f is the collection of all ordered pairs . In particular, graph means the graphical representation of this collection, in the form of a curve or surface, together with axes, etc. Graphing on a Cartesian plane is sometimes referred to as curve sketching.
    a. Thing
    b. Graph of a function0
    c. Undefined
    d. Undefined

41. In astronomy, geography, geometry and related sciences and contexts, a plane is said to be _____ at a given point if it is locally perpendicular to the gradient of the gravity field, i.e., with the direction of the gravitational force at that point.
    a. Horizontal0
    b. Thing
    c. Undefined
    d. Undefined

42. A _____ is a set of numbers that designate location in a given reference system, such as x,y in a planar _____ system or an x,y,z in a three-dimensional _____ system.
    a. Coordinate0
    b. Thing
    c. Undefined
    d. Undefined

43. In mathematics, the multiplicative inverse of a number x, denoted 1/x or x^{-1}, is the number which, when multiplied by x, yields 1. The multiplicative inverse of x is also called the _____ of x.
    a. Thing
    b. Reciprocal0
    c. Undefined
    d. Undefined

44. Deductive _____ is the kind of _____ in which the conclusion is necessitated by, or reached from, previously known facts (the premises).
    a. Thing
    b. Reasoning0
    c. Undefined
    d. Undefined

45. In Euclidean geometry, a uniform _____ is a linear transformation that enlargers or diminishes objects, and whose _____ factor is the same in all directions. This is also called homothethy.
    a. Thing
    b. Scale0
    c. Undefined
    d. Undefined

46. In mathematics, a _____ of a number x is the exponent y of the power by such that $x = b^y$. The value used for the base b must be neither 0 nor 1, nor a root of 1 in the case of the extension to complex numbers, and is typically 10, e, or 2.
    a. Logarithm0
    b. Thing
    c. Undefined
    d. Undefined

Chapter 9. Exponential and Logarithmic Functions

47. A _____ is a three-dimensional solid object bounded by six square faces, facets, or sides, with three meeting at each vertex.
    a. Thing
    b. Cube0
    c. Undefined
    d. Undefined

48. A _____ of a number is a number a such that $a^3 = x$.
    a. Cube root0
    b. Thing
    c. Undefined
    d. Undefined

49. A _____ is a set of possible values that a variable can take on in order to satisfy a given set of conditions, which may include equations and inequalities.
    a. Thing
    b. Solution set0
    c. Undefined
    d. Undefined

50. In mathematics, a _____ of a complex-valued function f is a member x of the domain of f such that f(x) vanishes at x, that is, x : f (x) = 0.
    a. Thing
    b. Root0
    c. Undefined
    d. Undefined

51. A _____ is a negotiable instrument instructing a financial institution to pay a specific amount of a specific currency from a specific demand account held in the maker/depositor's name with that institution. Both the maker and payee may be natural persons or legal entities.
    a. Thing
    b. Check0
    c. Undefined
    d. Undefined

52. _____ is a mathematical operation, written a^n, involving two numbers, the base a and the exponent n.
    a. Exponentiating0
    b. Thing
    c. Undefined
    d. Undefined

53. _____ is a mathematical operation, written a^n, involving two numbers, the base a and the exponent n.
    a. Thing
    b. Exponentiation0
    c. Undefined
    d. Undefined

54. Equivalence is the condition of being _____ or essentially equal.
    a. Equivalent0
    b. Thing
    c. Undefined
    d. Undefined

55. A _____ is a symbolic representation denoting a quantity or expression. It often represents an "unknown" quantity that has the potential to change.
    a. Thing
    b. Variable0
    c. Undefined
    d. Undefined

56. An _____ is a combination of numbers, operators, grouping symbols and/or free variables and bound variables arranged in a meaningful way which can be evaluated..

Chapter 9. Exponential and Logarithmic Functions

    a. Expression0   b. Thing
    c. Undefined   d. Undefined

57. In mathematics, an inequality is a statement about the relative size or order of two objects. For example 14 > 10, or 14 is _____ 10.
    a. Greater than0   b. Thing
    c. Undefined   d. Undefined

58. The _____ of a mathematical object is its size: a property by which it can be larger or smaller than other objects of the same kind; in technical terms, an ordering of the class of objects to which it belongs.
    a. Thing   b. Magnitude0
    c. Undefined   d. Undefined

59. The _____ is a nonnegative scalar measure of a wave's magnitude of oscillation, that is, the magnitude of the maximum disturbance in the medium during one wave cycle.
    a. Thing   b. Amplitude0
    c. Undefined   d. Undefined

60. An _____ is the result from the sudden release of stored energy in the Earth's crust that creates seismic waves.
    a. Thing   b. Earthquake0
    c. Undefined   d. Undefined

61. A _____ is a function that assigns a number to subsets of a given set.
    a. Measure0   b. Thing
    c. Undefined   d. Undefined

62. In mathematics, a _____ is the result of multiplying, or an expression that identifies factors to be multiplied.
    a. Thing   b. Product0
    c. Undefined   d. Undefined

63. A _____ is the result of the addition of a set of numbers. The numbers may be natural numbers, complex numbers, matrices, or still more complicated objects. An infinite _____ is a subtle procedure known as a series.
    a. Thing   b. Sum0
    c. Undefined   d. Undefined

64. In mathematics, a _____ is the end result of a division problem. It can also be expressed as the number of times the divisor divides into the dividend.
    a. Thing   b. Quotient0
    c. Undefined   d. Undefined

65. _____ has many meanings, most of which simply .
    a. Power0   b. Thing
    c. Undefined   d. Undefined

66. The _____ of an algebraic expression is the same equation, but without parentheses.

Chapter 9. Exponential and Logarithmic Functions

a. Expanded form0
b. Thing
c. Undefined
d. Undefined

67. _____, either of the curved-bracket punctuation marks that together make a set of _____
a. Thing
b. Parentheses0
c. Undefined
d. Undefined

68. A _____ is a number that is less than zero.
a. Thing
b. Negative number0
c. Undefined
d. Undefined

69. _____ is the chance that something is likely to happen or be the case.
a. Thing
b. Probability0
c. Undefined
d. Undefined

70. _____ are a measure of time.
a. Thing
b. Minutes0
c. Undefined
d. Undefined

71. A _____ is a quantity that denotes the proportional amount or magnitude of one quantity relative to another.
a. Thing
b. Ratio0
c. Undefined
d. Undefined

72. In mathematics, an _____, mean, or central tendency of a data set refers to a measure of the "middle" or "expected" value of the data set.
a. Average0
b. Concept
c. Undefined
d. Undefined

73. _____ is the logarithm to the base e, where e is an irrational constant approximately equal to 2.718281828459.
a. Thing
b. Natural logarithm0
c. Undefined
d. Undefined

74. In mathematics, the _____ is the logarithm with base 10.
a. Thing
b. Common logarithm0
c. Undefined
d. Undefined

75. _____ is a set of numbers, in the broadest sense of the word, together with one or more operations, such as addition or multiplication.
a. Thing
b. Number system0
c. Undefined
d. Undefined

76. The _____ of a ring R is defined to be the smallest positive integer n such that n a = 0, for all a in R.
a. Thing
b. Characteristic0
c. Undefined
d. Undefined

Chapter 9. Exponential and Logarithmic Functions

77. In mathematics, a _____ can mean either an element of the set {1, 2, 3, ...} (i.e the positive integers) or an element of the set {0, 1, 2, 3, ...} (i.e. the non-negative integers).
    a. Concept
    b. Whole number0
    c. Undefined
    d. Undefined

78. _____ is the process of reducing the number of significant digits in a number.
    a. Rounding0
    b. Concept
    c. Undefined
    d. Undefined

79. _____ is a notation for writing numbers that is often used by scientists and mathematicians to make it easier to write large and small numbers.
    a. Thing
    b. Scientific notation0
    c. Undefined
    d. Undefined

80. _____ is a term used in accounting, economics and finance with reference to the fact that assets with finite lives lose value over time.
    a. Depreciation0
    b. Thing
    c. Undefined
    d. Undefined

81. The _____ is the process of converting elements in one basis to another when both describe the same elements of the finite field $GF(p^m)$.
    a. Change of base0
    b. Thing
    c. Undefined
    d. Undefined

82. The _____ is the process of converting elements in one basis to another when both describe the same elements of the finite field $GF(p^m)$.
    a. Change of bases0
    b. Thing
    c. Undefined
    d. Undefined

83. The _____ is the period of time required for a quantity to double in size or value.
    a. Doubling time0
    b. Thing
    c. Undefined
    d. Undefined

84. In mathematics, a _____ is a demonstration that, assuming certain axioms, some statement is necessarily true.
    a. Proof0
    b. Thing
    c. Undefined
    d. Undefined

85. An _____ is an equality that remains true regardless of the values of any variables that appear within it, to distinguish it from an equality which is true under more particular conditions.
    a. Identity0
    b. Thing
    c. Undefined
    d. Undefined

86. In sociology and biology a _____ is the collection of people or organisms of a particular species living in a given geographic area or space, usually measured by a census.

Chapter 9. Exponential and Logarithmic Functions

    a. Thing
    c. Undefined
    b. Population0
    d. Undefined

87. In mathematics, the _____ of two sets A and B is the set that contains all elements of A that also belong to B (or equivalently, all elements of B that also belong to A), but no other elements.
    a. Intersection0
    c. Undefined
    b. Thing
    d. Undefined

88. _____ of an object is its speed in a particular direction.
    a. Velocity0
    c. Undefined
    b. Thing
    d. Undefined

89. In mathematics, a _____ may be described informally as a number that can be given by an infinite decimal representation.
    a. Thing
    c. Undefined
    b. Real number0
    d. Undefined

90. A _____ is the part of a fraction that tells how many equal parts make up a whole, and which is used in the name of the fraction: "halves", "thirds", "fourths" or "quarters", "fifths" and so on.
    a. Concept
    c. Undefined
    b. Denominator0
    d. Undefined

91. In mathematics, an _____ is a statement about the relative size or order of two objects.
    a. Inequality0
    c. Undefined
    b. Thing
    d. Undefined

92. _____ is often used to describe the measurement of the steepness, incline, gradient, or grade of a straight line. The _____ is defined as the ratio of the "rise" divided by the "run" between two points on a line, or in other words, the ratio of the altitude change to the horizontal distance between any two points on the line.
    a. Slope0
    c. Undefined
    b. Thing
    d. Undefined

93. _____ are objects, characters, or other concrete representations of ideas, concepts, or other abstractions.
    a. Thing
    c. Undefined
    b. Symbols0
    d. Undefined

94. In plane geometry, a _____ is a polygon with four equal sides, four right angles, and parallel opposite sides. In algebra, the _____ of a number is that number multiplied by itself.
    a. Square0
    c. Undefined
    b. Thing
    d. Undefined

95. In mathematics, a _____ of a number x is a number r such that $r^2 = x$, or in words, a number r whose square (the result of multiplying the number by itself) is x.
    a. Square root0
    c. Undefined
    b. Thing
    d. Undefined

Chapter 9. Exponential and Logarithmic Functions

96. In mathematics and logic, a _____ proof is a way of showing the truth or falsehood of a given statement by a straightforward combination of established facts, usually existing lemmas and theorems, without making any further assumptions.
   a. Thing
   b. Direct0
   c. Undefined
   d. Undefined

97. _____ is the relationship between two variables, like a ratio in which the two quantities being compared are different units.
   a. Direct variation0
   b. Thing
   c. Undefined
   d. Undefined

98. In mathematics, a _____ set is the complement of a meager set. A meager set is one which is the countable union of nowhere dense sets.
   a. Thing
   b. Residual0
   c. Undefined
   d. Undefined

99. The word _____ comes from the Latin word linearis, which means created by lines.
   a. Linear0
   b. Thing
   c. Undefined
   d. Undefined

100. In mathematical logic, a Gödel numbering (or Gödel _____) is a function that assigns to each symbol and well-formed formula of some formal language a unique natural number called its Gödel number.
   a. Code0
   b. Thing
   c. Undefined
   d. Undefined

Chapter 10. Conic Sections

1. A <U>circle</U> is a series of points the same distance from a given point, called the center.
   a. -equivalence
   b. Circle10
   c. Undefined
   d. Undefined

2. An <U>equation</U> is represented by two expressions that have the same value.
   a. Equation10
   b. ADE classification
   c. Undefined
   d. Undefined

3. The word _____ can have three meanings: In _____ theory, a _____ is an abstract object consisting of vertices (or nodes) and edges (or arcs) between pairs of vertices. The _____ of a function f : X ¨ Y is the set of all pairs (x,f(x)) The _____ of a relation, a generalisation of the _____ of a function.
   a. -equivalence
   b. Graph10
   c. Undefined
   d. Undefined

4. A _____ is an undefined term. However, it is often thought of as a series of points. A _____ has one dimension - length. A _____ is either named by a lower case letter or by two points on the _____.
   a. Line10
   b. -equivalence
   c. Undefined
   d. Undefined

5. The <U>radius</U> of a circle is the distance from the center to the circle.
   a. Radius10
   b. -equivalence
   c. Undefined
   d. Undefined

6. The point of intersection of the horizontal and vertical axes in the rectangular coordinate plane is the _____. It is is expressed as the ordered pair (0,0).
   a. Origin10
   b. ADE classification
   c. Undefined
   d. Undefined

7. The <U>diameter</U> of a circle is a chord that goes through the center.
   a. -equivalence
   b. Diameter10
   c. Undefined
   d. Undefined

8. A <U>plane</U> is an undefined term. We can think of it as a series of lines having 2 dimensions, width and length.
   a. -equivalence
   b. Plane10
   c. Undefined
   d. Undefined

9. The _____ is the distance around a closed curve. _____ is a kind of perimeter.
   a. -equivalence
   b. Circumference10
   c. Undefined
   d. Undefined

10. A measure of variability, the _____ is the distance from the lowest to the highest score.
    a. Range10
    b. -equivalence
    c. Undefined
    d. Undefined

11. A quadrilateral with opposite sides equal and parallel and containing all right angles is called a <U>rectangle.</U>

Chapter 10. Conic Sections 123

   a. -equivalence
   b. Rectangle10
   c. Undefined
   d. Undefined

12. The <U>opposite </U>of a number is the number that makes a sum zero. In most cases, this means just to change the sign. 3 is the _____ of -3.
   a. ADE classification
   b. Opposite10
   c. Undefined
   d. Undefined

13. An _____ is one of the number lines found on the rectangular coordinate system. The x asis is the horizontal number line while the y _____ is the vertical number line.
   a. Axis10
   b. ADE classification
   c. Undefined
   d. Undefined

14. An _____ combines numbers, operators, and/or variables but contains no equal or inequality sign.
   a. Expression10
   b. ADE classification
   c. Undefined
   d. Undefined

15. A <U>point </U>is an undefined term. We usually represent this by a dot, but a _____ actually has no dimension. A capital letter names any _____.
   a. -equivalence
   b. Point10
   c. Undefined
   d. Undefined

16. A _____ is a well-defined collection of objects considered as a whole.
   a. -equivalence
   b. Set10
   c. Undefined
   d. Undefined

17. A set of numbers that satisfies a given equation or inequality is a _____.
   a. Solution set10
   b. -equivalence
   c. Undefined
   d. Undefined

18. Addition (or summation) is one of the basic operations of arithmetic. In its simplest form, addition combines two numbers, the augend and addend, into a single number, the _____. Adding more numbers can be viewed as repeated addition. (Repeated addition of the number one is the most basic form of counting.) By extension, the addition of zero numbers, one number, or infinitely many numbers can be defined.
   a. Sum10
   b. -equivalence
   c. Undefined
   d. Undefined

19. The answer to subtraction is called the <U>difference</U>.
   a. Difference10
   b. -equivalence
   c. Undefined
   d. Undefined

20. The axes in a rectangular coordinate systems naturally cuts the plane into 4 separate regions called <U>quadrants.</U>These are usually represented by Roman Numerals starting with the upper right quadrant.
   a. Quadrants10
   b. -equivalence
   c. Undefined
   d. Undefined

21. _____ is the change in y between two points.
   a. -equivalence
   b. Rise10
   c. Undefined
   d. Undefined

22. A number that does not change in value in a given situation is a _____.
   a. Constant10
   b. -equivalence
   c. Undefined
   d. Undefined

23. A <U>line segment </U>is a piece of a line. The _____ has definite length and is named by the two endpoints.
   a. Line segment10
   b. -equivalence
   c. Undefined
   d. Undefined

ANSWER KEY

Chapter 1

1. b	2. b	3. a	4. a	5. b	6. b	7. a	8. a	9. a	10. a
11. b	12. a	13. a	14. b	15. b	16. b	17. a	18. a	19. b	20. a
21. a	22. b	23. b	24. a	25. b	26. a	27. b	28. b	29. a	30. b
31. b	32. b	33. a	34. b	35. a	36. b	37. b	38. b	39. a	40. a
41. b	42. b	43. b	44. b	45. a	46. b	47. b	48. a	49. a	50. b
51. b	52. a	53. b	54. b	55. a	56. a	57. a	58. b	59. a	60. b
61. b	62. b	63. b	64. b	65. a	66. a	67. a	68. a	69. a	70. b
71. b	72. b	73. b	74. a	75. b	76. a	77. b	78. a	79. b	80. a
81. b	82. b	83. a	84. a	85. b	86. b	87. a	88. b	89. a	90. a
91. b	92. b	93. b	94. b	95. b	96. a	97. a	98. a	99. b	100. a
101. a	102. a	103. a	104. b	105. a	106. a	107. b	108. b	109. a	110. a
111. a	112. a	113. b	114. b	115. a	116. a	117. a	118. b	119. b	120. b
121. a	122. b	123. a	124. b	125. b	126. b	127. a	128. a	129. b	130. b
131. a	132. b	133. a	134. b	135. b	136. a	137. b	138. a	139. a	140. b
141. a									

Chapter 2

1. b	2. a	3. a	4. b	5. a	6. a	7. b	8. b	9. b	10. b
11. b	12. a	13. b	14. a	15. b	16. a	17. a	18. b	19. b	20. b
21. a	22. b	23. b	24. a	25. a	26. a	27. b	28. a	29. a	30. b
31. b	32. a	33. b	34. a	35. b	36. b	37. b	38. a	39. a	40. a
41. b	42. a	43. a	44. b	45. a	46. b	47. a	48. a	49. b	50. b
51. a	52. b	53. b	54. a	55. b	56. a	57. b	58. b	59. a	60. b
61. b	62. a	63. b	64. b	65. b	66. a	67. b	68. b	69. b	70. b
71. b	72. a	73. a	74. a	75. b	76. b	77. b	78. b	79. a	80. a
81. a	82. a	83. b	84. b	85. a	86. a	87. b	88. a	89. a	90. a
91. b	92. b	93. a	94. b	95. b	96. a	97. a	98. a	99. a	100. b
101. a	102. b	103. b	104. a	105. a	106. b	107. b	108. b	109. a	110. a
111. a	112. a	113. b	114. b	115. a	116. b	117. b	118. b	119. b	120. a
121. b	122. a	123. b	124. b						

Chapter 3

1. a	2. a	3. b	4. b	5. a	6. b	7. a	8. b	9. b	10. a
11. a	12. b	13. a	14. a	15. b	16. b	17. a	18. b	19. b	20. a
21. a	22. a	23. a	24. a	25. b	26. b	27. b	28. b	29. a	30. b
31. a	32. b	33. a	34. b	35. b	36. a	37. a	38. a	39. b	40. a
41. a	42. a	43. a	44. a	45. a	46. b	47. b	48. a	49. a	50. b
51. b	52. a	53. a	54. a	55. a	56. b	57. a	58. a	59. b	60. a
61. b	62. b	63. a	64. b	65. a	66. b	67. a	68. b	69. a	70. a
71. b	72. a	73. b	74. b	75. b	76. b	77. b	78. a	79. a	80. a
81. a	82. b	83. a	84. a	85. b	86. b	87. b	88. a	89. a	90. a
91. a	92. a	93. a	94. b	95. b	96. b	97. a	98. a	99. b	100. a
101. b	102. b	103. a	104. a	105. a	106. b	107. b	108. b	109. a	110. b
111. b	112. a	113. a	114. b	115. b	116. b	117. a	118. b	119. b	120. b
121. b	122. b	123. a	124. b	125. a	126. a	127. b	128. a	129. b	130. a
131. a	132. a	133. b	134. b	135. a	136. b	137. b	138. b	139. a	140. a
141. a	142. a	143. b	144. b	145. b	146. a	147. b	148. b	149. a	150. b
151. a	152. a	153. b	154. b						

Chapter 4

1. a	2. b	3. a	4. b	5. a	6. b	7. b	8. b	9. a	10. a
11. b	12. a	13. a	14. a	15. b	16. b	17. a	18. a	19. a	20. a
21. b	22. b	23. a	24. b	25. a	26. a	27. a	28. a	29. a	30. a
31. b	32. a	33. b	34. a	35. a	36. b	37. b	38. b	39. a	40. b
41. a	42. a	43. a	44. b	45. b	46. b	47. b	48. b	49. a	50. b
51. b	52. b	53. a	54. a	55. b	56. b	57. b	58. a	59. a	60. b
61. a	62. b	63. b	64. a	65. a	66. a	67. b	68. b	69. b	70. a
71. b	72. b	73. b	74. a	75. b	76. a	77. a	78. b	79. a	80. a
81. a	82. b	83. b	84. a	85. b	86. b	87. b	88. b	89. b	90. b
91. b	92. b	93. b	94. a	95. b	96. b	97. a	98. a	99. a	100. b
101. b	102. a	103. a	104. b	105. a	106. b				

Chapter 5

1. b	2. b	3. a	4. b	5. a	6. a	7. a	8. a	9. b	10. a
11. b	12. b	13. b	14. b	15. a	16. b	17. b	18. a	19. b	20. a
21. a	22. a	23. b	24. b	25. a	26. b	27. a	28. b	29. a	30. b
31. a	32. a	33. a	34. b	35. b	36. a	37. a	38. b	39. b	40. b
41. a	42. a	43. a	44. a	45. b	46. a	47. a	48. a	49. b	50. b
51. a	52. a	53. b	54. b	55. a	56. b	57. b	58. a	59. b	60. a
61. b	62. a	63. b	64. b	65. a	66. a	67. b	68. b	69. b	70. a
71. b	72. a	73. a	74. b	75. b	76. a	77. b	78. a	79. b	80. b
81. b	82. b	83. a	84. b	85. b	86. a	87. b	88. b	89. b	90. b
91. a	92. b	93. a	94. b	95. b	96. a	97. b	98. a	99. b	100. b
101. a	102. a	103. a	104. a	105. a	106. b	107. b	108. a	109. a	110. a
111. b	112. a	113. b	114. b	115. a	116. a	117. a	118. b	119. b	120. b
121. a	122. b	123. b	124. a						

ANSWER KEY

Chapter 6

1. a	2. b	3. b	4. b	5. b	6. b	7. b	8. a	9. a	10. b
11. b	12. b	13. b	14. b	15. a	16. a	17. a	18. b	19. b	20. a
21. a	22. b	23. b	24. b	25. a	26. a	27. a	28. a	29. b	30. a
31. b	32. b	33. a	34. a	35. a	36. a	37. a	38. a	39. a	40. a
41. b	42. b	43. a	44. a	45. a	46. a	47. b	48. a	49. a	50. b
51. a	52. b	53. b	54. b	55. b	56. a	57. b	58. a	59. b	60. b
61. a	62. a	63. b	64. b	65. a	66. b	67. b	68. b	69. a	70. b
71. a	72. b	73. b	74. b	75. a	76. a	77. a	78. b	79. a	80. a
81. b	82. b	83. b	84. b	85. a	86. a	87. b	88. b	89. a	90. a
91. a	92. b	93. a	94. a	95. a	96. a	97. b	98. a	99. b	100. a
101. a	102. b	103. a	104. b	105. b	106. b	107. b	108. b	109. b	110. b
111. b	112. b	113. a	114. b	115. a	116. b				

Chapter 7

1. b	2. b	3. b	4. a	5. a	6. b	7. a	8. b	9. b	10. a
11. a	12. b	13. a	14. b	15. a	16. a	17. a	18. b	19. b	20. a
21. a	22. b	23. a	24. a	25. b	26. b	27. b	28. b	29. b	30. a
31. a	32. b	33. b	34. a	35. a	36. b	37. b	38. a	39. a	40. b
41. a	42. a	43. a	44. b	45. a	46. b	47. a	48. a	49. b	50. a
51. a	52. b	53. a	54. a	55. a	56. a	57. b	58. a	59. b	60. a
61. b	62. a	63. a	64. a	65. b	66. b	67. a	68. b	69. a	70. a
71. a	72. a	73. a	74. b	75. a	76. b	77. a	78. b	79. b	80. a
81. b	82. b	83. b	84. b	85. a	86. a	87. b	88. a	89. a	90. b
91. a	92. b	93. a	94. b	95. a	96. a	97. b	98. a	99. b	100. a
101. a	102. a	103. b	104. b	105. b	106. a	107. b	108. b	109. b	110. a
111. b	112. b	113. b	114. b	115. a	116. a	117. a	118. b	119. b	120. a
121. b	122. b	123. a	124. a	125. a	126. a	127. b	128. b	129. b	130. b
131. a	132. b	133. a	134. a	135. b	136. a	137. b	138. a	139. a	140. b
141. a	142. a	143. b	144. a	145. a	146. a				

Chapter 8

1. b	2. a	3. a	4. a	5. a	6. b	7. b	8. a	9. a	10. b
11. a	12. b	13. b	14. b	15. a	16. b	17. a	18. a	19. b	20. b
21. b	22. b	23. b	24. a	25. a	26. b	27. b	28. b	29. b	30. b
31. a	32. b	33. b	34. a	35. a	36. b	37. a	38. b	39. b	40. a
41. a	42. a	43. a	44. a	45. b	46. a	47. a	48. b	49. b	50. a
51. a	52. a	53. a	54. b	55. a	56. a	57. b	58. b	59. b	60. b
61. b	62. b	63. b	64. b	65. b	66. b	67. b	68. a	69. b	70. a
71. b	72. b	73. b	74. b	75. a	76. b	77. b	78. a	79. a	80. a
81. a	82. b	83. a	84. b	85. a	86. a	87. b	88. b	89. a	90. b
91. b	92. b	93. a	94. b	95. b	96. b	97. b	98. a	99. b	100. a
101. a	102. b	103. a							

Chapter 9

1. b	2. b	3. a	4. a	5. b	6. b	7. a	8. b	9. b	10. b
11. a	12. b	13. b	14. a	15. a	16. a	17. b	18. b	19. b	20. a
21. b	22. a	23. b	24. b	25. a	26. b	27. a	28. a	29. a	30. b
31. a	32. a	33. a	34. a	35. b	36. b	37. a	38. b	39. b	40. b
41. a	42. a	43. b	44. b	45. b	46. a	47. b	48. a	49. b	50. b
51. b	52. a	53. b	54. a	55. b	56. a	57. a	58. b	59. b	60. b
61. a	62. b	63. b	64. b	65. a	66. a	67. b	68. b	69. b	70. b
71. b	72. a	73. b	74. b	75. b	76. b	77. b	78. a	79. b	80. a
81. a	82. a	83. a	84. a	85. a	86. b	87. a	88. a	89. a	90. b
91. a	92. a	93. b	94. a	95. a	96. b	97. a	98. b	99. a	100. a

Chapter 10

1. b	2. a	3. b	4. a	5. a	6. a	7. b	8. b	9. b	10. a
11. b	12. b	13. a	14. a	15. b	16. b	17. a	18. a	19. a	20. a
21. b	22. a	23. a							